ISBN 0-8373-6761-1

CS-61 GENERAL APTITUDE AND ABILITIES SERIES

This is your
PASSBOOK® for...

In-Basket Examination

Test Preparation Study Guide

Questions & Answers

NLC

NATIONAL LEARNING CORPORATION

PASSBOOK®

NOTICE

This book is *SOLELY* intended for, is sold *ONLY* to, and its use is *RESTRICTED* to *individual*, bona fide applicants or candidates who qualify by virtue of having seriously filed applications for appropriate license, certificate, professional and/or promotional advancement, higher school matriculation, scholarship, or other legitimate requirements of educational and/or governmental authorities.

This book is *NOT* intended for use, class instruction, tutoring, training, duplication, copying, reprinting, excerption, or adaptation, etc., by:

(1) Other publishers

(2) Proprietors and/or Instructors of "Coaching" and/or Preparatory Courses

(3) Personnel and/or Training Divisions of commercial, industrial, and governmental organizations

(4) Schools, colleges, or universities and/or their departments and staffs, including teachers and other personnel

(5) Testing Agencies or Bureaus

(6) Study groups which seek by the purchase of a single volume to copy and/or duplicate and/or adapt this material for use by the group as a whole without having purchased individual volumes for each of the members of the group

(7) Et al.

Such persons would be in violation of appropriate Federal and State statutes.

PROVISION OF LICENSING AGREEMENTS. — Recognized educational commercial, industrial, and governmental institutions and organizations, and others legitimately engaged in educational pursuits, including training, testing, and measurement activities, may address a request for a licensing agreement to the copyright owners, who will determine whether, and under what conditions, including fees and charges, the materials in this book may be used by them. In other words, a licensing facility exists for the legitimate use of the material in this book on other than an individual basis. However, it is asseverated and affirmed here that the material in this book *CANNOT* be used without the receipt of the express permission of such a licensing agreement from the Publishers.

NATIONAL LEARNING CORPORATION
212 Michael Drive
Syosset, New York 11791

Inquiries re licensing agreements should be addressed to:
The President
National Learning Corporation
212 Michael Drive
Syosset, New York 11791

PASSBOOK SERIES®

THE *PASSBOOK SERIES®* has been created to prepare applicants and candidates for the ultimate academic battlefield – the examination room.

At some time in our lives, each and every one of us may be required to take an examination – for validation, matriculation, admission, qualification, registration, certification, or licensure.

Based on the assumption that every applicant or candidate has met the basic formal educational standards, has taken the required number of courses, and read the necessary texts, the *PASSBOOK SERIES®* furnishes the one special preparation which may assure passing with confidence, instead of failing with insecurity. Examination questions – together with answers – are furnished as the basic vehicle for study so that the mysteries of the examination and its compounding difficulties may be eliminated or diminished by a sure method.

This book is meant to help you pass your examination provided that you qualify and are serious in your objective.

The entire field is reviewed through the huge store of content information which is succinctly presented through a provocative and challenging approach – the question-and-answer method.

A climate of success is established by furnishing the correct answers at the end of each test.

You soon learn to recognize types of questions, forms of questions, and patterns of questioning. You may even begin to anticipate expected outcomes.

You perceive that many questions are repeated or adapted so that you can gain acute insights, which may enable you to score many sure points.

You learn how to confront new questions, or types of questions, and to attack them confidently and work out the correct answers.

You note objectives and emphases, and recognize pitfalls and dangers, so that you may make positive educational adjustments.

Moreover, you are kept fully informed in relation to new concepts, methods, practices, and directions in the field.

You discover that you are actually taking the examination all the time: you are preparing for the examination by "taking" an examination, not by reading extraneous and/or supererogatory textbooks.

In short, this PASSBOOK®, used directedly, should be an important factor in helping you to pass your test.

THE "IN-BASKET" EXAMINATION

While the exact format of in-basket exercises will vary, they frequently involve each trainee in a group first individually assuming the role of a manager who is faced with a number of letters, memoirs, and notes to which he must respond in writing within a limited time period. For example, the trainee may be told that he has just returned from vacation and that he must leave on a trip in four hours, during which time he must respond in writing to all the items on his desk.

To further complicate the exercise, you, the trainee, may be told that you have just returned from vacation and must leave on a business trip in five hours. Also, it is a holiday and your secretary is home, and no one else is around the office to help you. There are more inquiries and problems to respond to than is possible in five hours and so you will have to determine the relative priority of the work to be done.

As you can see, the IN-BASKET EXERCISE demands good decision-making skills, rather than learning new facts or acquiring new skills. The time pressure factor may result in your finding out how well you perform under stress.

When these exercises are conducted in an oral format, and after each exercise is finished (time runs out), you may be asked to justify your decisions and actions to the examiner and the other participants when it is held as a group exercise, and then they in turn will evaluate your actions and critique it. The rating, of course, is done differently in competitive examinations.

The fact that this type of exercise can be given to groups of managerial trainees is considered an advantage to management, i.e., it is easier and cheaper to administer than other training methods. This training technique also tests managerial candidates for decision-making abilities, particularly due to the time constraints involved. This is considered a vital skill for most managerial candidates for decision-making abilities, particularly due to the time constraints involved. This is considered a vital skill for most managerial positions and, although other training techniques such as role playing can also provide stress, in-basket exercises do more so and are specifically designed for this purpose.

There are limitations, too. As with in-basket questions pertaining to case study examples, they are in large part hypothetical in nature, or static, in that the managerial candidate does not have to live or "die" with the consequences of a poor decision, except where he/she is rated poorly on an examination.

Some in-basket exercises provide guidelines or suggestions for solution. The candidate may be presented with a problem which requires a series of decisions and actions but is also presented with a number of alternate means of resolving the problem, from which he must choose the best option. Next, the problem may be further developed and you may be provided with a number of new choices to resolve this new, or expanded, problem. It may even be required a third time. Then comes the evaluation and critique.

So with this technique, the trainee receives information evaluating the consequences, good or bad, of his decisions at each decision point in the exercise.

In order to properly critique the trainee's decisions, the examiner must be highly skilled in conducting the exercise and in conducting the critique. At its extremes, the critique, as with performance evaluations, can be so general as to be meaningless or be so specific that the trainee becomes so overwhelmed as to render the whole training exercise pointless.

In-basket exercises are often used in on-the-job management group training programs, together with case studies.

HOW TO TAKE A TEST

You have studied long, hard and conscientiously.

With your official admission card in hand, and your heart pounding, you have been admitted to the examination room.

You note that there are several hundred other applicants in the examination room waiting to take the same test.

They all appear to be equally well prepared.

You know that nothing but your best effort will suffice. The "moment of truth" is at hand: you now have to demonstrate objectively, in writing, your knowledge of content and your understanding of subject matter.

You are fighting the most important battle of your life—to pass and/or score high on an examination which will determine your career and provide the economic basis for your livelihood.

What extra, special things should you know and should you do in taking the examination?

BEFORE THE TEST

YOUR PHYSICAL CONDITION IS IMPORTANT

If you are not well, you can't do your best work on tests. If you are half asleep, you can't do your best either. Here are some tips:

1) Get about the same amount of sleep you usually get. Don't stay up all night before the test, either partying or worrying—DON'T DO IT!
2) If you wear glasses, be sure to wear them when you go to take the test. This goes for hearing aids, too.
3) If you have any physical problems that may keep you from doing your best, be sure to tell the person giving the test. If you are sick or in poor health, you really cannot do your best on any test. You can always come back and take the test some other time.

AT THE TEST

EXAMINATION TECHNIQUES

1) Read the general instructions carefully. These are usually printed on the first page of the exam booklet. As a rule, these instructions refer to the timing of the examination; the fact that you should not start work until the signal and must stop work at a signal, etc. If there are any *special* instructions, such as a choice of questions to be answered, make sure that you note this instruction carefully.

2) When you are ready to start work on the examination, that is as soon as the signal has been given, read the instructions to each question booklet, underline any key words or phrases, such as *least, best, outline, describe* and the like. In this way you will tend to answer as requested rather than discover on reviewing your paper that you *listed without describing*, that you selected the *worst* choice rather than the *best* choice, etc.

3) If the examination is of the objective or multiple-choice type – that is, each question will also give a series of possible answers: A, B, C or D, and you are called upon to select the best answer and write the letter next to that answer on your answer paper – it is advisable to start answering each question in turn. There may be anywhere from 50 to 100 such questions in the three or four hours allotted and you can see how much time would be taken if you read through all the questions before beginning to answer any. Furthermore, if you come across a question or group of questions which you know would be difficult to answer, it would undoubtedly affect your handling of all the other questions.

4) If the examination is of the essay type and contains but a few questions, it is a moot point as to whether you should read all the questions before starting to answer any one. Of course, if you are given a choice – say five out of seven and the like – then it is essential to read all the questions so you can eliminate the two which are most difficult. If, however, you are asked to answer all the questions, there may be danger in trying to answer the easiest one first because you may find that you will spend too much time on it. The best technique is to answer the first question, then proceed to the second, etc.

5) Time your answers. Before the exam begins, write down the time it started, then add the time allowed for the examination and write down the time it must be completed, then divide the time available somewhat as follows:
   - If 3-1/2 hours are allowed, that would be 210 minutes. If you have 80 objective-type questions, that would be an average of 2-1/2 minutes per question. Allow yourself no more than 2 minutes per question, or a total of 160 minutes, which will permit about 50 minutes to review.
   - If for the time allotment of 210 minutes there are 7 essay questions to answer, that would average about 30 minutes a question. Give yourself only 25 minutes per question so that you have about 35 minutes to review.

6) The most important instruction is to *read each question* and make sure you know what is wanted. The second most important instruction is to *time yourself properly* so that you answer every question. The third most important instruction is to *answer every question*. Guess if you have to but include something for each question. Remember that you will receive no credit for a blank and will probably receive some credit if you write something in answer to an essay question. If you guess a letter – say "B" for a multiple-choice question – you may have guessed right. If you leave a blank as an answer to a multiple-choice question, the examiners may respect your

feelings but it will not add a point to your score. Some exams may penalize you for wrong answers, so in such cases *only*, you may not want to guess unless you have some basis for your answer.

7) Suggestions
  a. Objective-type questions
      1. Examine the question booklet for proper sequence of pages and questions
      2. Read all instructions carefully
      3. Skip any question which seems too difficult; return to it after all other questions have been answered
      4. Apportion your time properly; do not spend too much time on any single question or group of questions
      5. Note and underline key words – *all, most, fewest, least, best, worst, same, opposite,* etc.
      6. Pay particular attention to negatives
      7. Note unusual option, e.g., unduly long, short, complex, different or similar in content to the body of the question
      8. Observe the use of "hedging" words – *probably, may, most likely,* etc.
      9. Make sure that your answer is put next to the same number as the question
      10. Do not second-guess unless you have good reason to believe the second answer is definitely more correct
      11. Cross out original answer if you decide another answer is more accurate; do not erase until you are ready to hand your paper in
      12. Answer all questions; guess unless instructed otherwise
      13. Leave time for review

  b. Essay questions
      1. Read each question carefully
      2. Determine exactly what is wanted. Underline key words or phrases.
      3. Decide on outline or paragraph answer
      4. Include many different points and elements unless asked to develop any one or two points or elements
      5. Show impartiality by giving pros and cons unless directed to select one side only
      6. Make and write down any assumptions you find necessary to answer the questions
      7. Watch your English, grammar, punctuation and choice of words
      8. Time your answers; don't crowd material

8) Answering the essay question

Most essay questions can be answered by framing the specific response around several key words or ideas. Here are a few such key words or ideas:

M's: manpower, materials, methods, money, management
P's: purpose, program, policy, plan, procedure, practice, problems, pitfalls, personnel, public relations

a. Six basic steps in handling problems:
   1. Preliminary plan and background development
   2. Collect information, data and facts
   3. Analyze and interpret information, data and facts
   4. Analyze and develop solutions as well as make recommendations
   5. Prepare report and sell recommendations
   6. Install recommendations and follow up effectiveness

b. Pitfalls to avoid
   1. *Taking things for granted* – A statement of the situation does not necessarily imply that each of the elements is necessarily true; for example, a complaint may be invalid and biased so that all that can be taken for granted is that a complaint has been registered
   2. *Considering only one side of a situation* – Wherever possible, indicate several alternatives and then point out the reasons you selected the best one
   3. *Failing to indicate follow up* – Whenever your answer indicates action on your part, make certain that you will take proper follow-up action to see how successful your recommendations, procedures or actions turn out to be
   4. *Taking too long in answering any single question* – Remember to time your answers properly

EXAMINATION SECTION

IN-BASKET EXERCISE

SAMPLE TEST QUESTIONS

These questions consist of a scenario in which the test taker assumes the role of a supervisor returning from a vacation and reviewing memos and analyzing the situations, identifying relationships, and making connections among the pieces of information provided in the scenario and in-basket items. These questions relate to the test taker's solution, decision or action in response to a problem to achieve a specific objective.

You are to read the situation described below and the three numbered in-basket items that follow. Then respond to the three multiple-choice questions that follow the in-basket materials.

Scenario and Background

Assume that you are Casey Jones, a District Sales Supervisor in the Sales Division of a major pharmaceutical company.

You supervise a staff of three Sales Representatives, each of whom leads a professional team that includes two assistant representatives. Your immediate supervisor is the District Manager of the Sales Division, Terry Gibson. The Sales Division also includes two other Supervisors and their staffs.

Your Sales Representatives and their assignments are:

Scott Bailey, Sales Area One
Jesse Taylor, Sales Area Two
Shawn Richard, Sales Area Three

Scott is your most experienced and competent employee. Jesse was transferred to you from another Sales District about one year ago, and Shawn is your newest employee who is very competent, but still is working on being an effective team leader.

It is Monday morning, April 12, and you have just returned from a one-week vacation. The numbered items that follow represent the contents of your in-basket. These include memos, letters, and other information that came in while you were on vacation. Your plan for the morning is to review and take action on your in-basket items. In about an hour, you will go to the first of several meetings that will consume the remainder of the day.

Interoffice Memo #1

Date: Tuesday, April 6th

From: Scott Bailey
          District Sales Representative, Area One

To: Casey Jones
          District Sales Supervisor
          Northeastern District

Subject: New Hires Training Program

Before you left, you approved the idea I had for the new training program and told me to proceed to order the new assimilation computers. However, the computer company, Technologies Expanding, assured me that they would arrive in time for our new hires to begin training. As you are aware, the training begins in one week, but I have not received the new computers yet. The customer service representative told me that the company has been having difficulties getting their orders out and could not guarantee that the computers would be in on time.

There is another company that can supply our computers, but the cost would be an additional $8,000. I recommend that we order from the other company and begin training on the old computers while we wait for the new computers. Although the new hires will not work on specific training for two weeks, we can at least start them on the product information part of the course.

Interoffice Memo #2

Date: Thursday, April 8th

From: Terry Gibson
          District Division Manager

To: Casey Jones
          District Sales Supervisor
          Northeastern District

Subject: New Company Policy

Beginning May 1st, there will be a new policy which requires all Sales Representative to have their clients fill out and sign the Form 2030. This form is for our inventory purposes. We had discussed using this form a couple of months ago and at the time found it to be quite tedious. But as our business is expanding and we are moving to other parts of the country, we need a more efficient way to keep track of what we are selling.

Our next inventory will be on May 30th. These forms must be filled out no later than May 15th so we can have the information to have a successful inventory. I know this is short notice, but it shouldn't long to go through your records of what your representatives have sold in the last six months. If you have any further questions or need any assistance you can contact my Administrative Assistant, Aaron Daigle, (x3632), who is collecting all the information.

Interoffice Memo #3

Date: Monday, April 5th

From: Jody Rogers
          Assistant District Sales Representative, Area Four

To: Casey Jones
          District Sales Supervisor
          Northeastern District

Subject: Area Team Four

I am requesting an assignment to a different Area Team. I have been working on Shawn Richard's team for the past six months. I realize that Shawn is a new employee and has only been in this position for seven months, but he does not handle leadership in a professional manner.

He is not organized, and I feel that Dale Stevens and I are the ones who are compensating for him. He does not delegate responsibility and cannot manage the travel schedule, the appointments, or the distribution lists. I have tried to help him get organized while Dale helps with the arrangements, but our efforts have not helped. He cannot seem to manage his time effectively, which leaves his assistants, me and Dale, to keep our area serviced.

How am I ever going to move up professionally and to show my talents if my work is suffering due to Shawn's inability to manage his team?

In-Basket Questions

1. Which of the following is the most appropriate action to take in response to the issue of the training schedule in Item #1?

   A. Allow Scott to proceed with the training on the old computers and then interrupt training when the new computers arrive.
   B. Delay the training till the new computers arrive.
   C. Let the students finish the course with the old computers without the interruption of the new computers, and the next group of students will begin training with the new computers.
   D. Cancel the training altogether until the issue with the computers has been resolved.

2. Which of the following actions will have the best resolution to the problem with Technologies Expanding?

   A. Cancel the order with Technologies Expanding and proceed with the new order.
   B. Contact the president of Technologies Expanding and demand a discount because the company did not meet your expectations.
   C. Cancel the order and have the old computers updated.
   D. Call the customer service representative manager to verify the accuracy of the information Scott received and discuss your situation and the options that are available to you.

3. What would be the best action to take in response to Jody's compliant? (Item #3)

   A. No action is required because Jody tends to exaggerate.
   B. Tell Jody that it is important to be supportive of each other and you will enroll her in a teambuilding course.
   C. Move Jody to Scott's team so she can help with the training.
   D. Look into the matter and see if there is evidence of Shawn's behavior described by Jody, and also talk with Dale to gain further insight into the issue.

KEY (CORRECT ANSWERS)

1. C – The students will get the training they need to perform the duties of the job without the interruption of the installation of the new computers.
2. D – By calling the service manager you can get a better idea of exactly what the situation is and what options are available to you before you cancel the order.
3. D – You first need to determine if there is a valid complaint and if Shawn's behavior reflects Jody's complaint before you take any action.

Senior Technical Writer/Content Director, Interaxion

You are T. SMITH, the senior technical writer/content director for an eight-year-old business service provider, Interaxion. The primary services provided to its clients are Web hosting, security services, high-capacity Internet access, and information system audits. You and your staff of 4 writers and 2 assistants have recently completed a draft of customer use manuals for a new addition to the service line: a dedicated storage network for clients with large amounts of data. Within the next several months, Interaxion also intends to launch a new download hosting service that will help clients place large files and applications on their own dedicated servers for access.

Interaxion is a medium-sized company that aggressively competes with larger business-to-business service organizations, much of them sprung from existing computer or telecommunications companies. To hold its market share, Interaxion offers a level of service and individual client attention that goes beyond the norm.

The president and CEO of your company, Marlane Liddell, is the engine behind Interaxion's aggressive approach. She is anxious to make Interaxion into a one-stop destination for any and all business-to-business networking services, which explains the rapid schedule of new product/service rollouts—now occurring at a pace of nearly two per year. Many employees privately complain that the grueling pace of development and launch makes work more stressful and error-prone, but the business is growing steadily. While some errors do occur in implementing and documenting services, the departments are managed well enough to correct these mistakes before they cause a significant loss of up-time for clients—if they weren't managed this well, Interaxion would have real problems in customer relations.

As the head of the technical writing department, you are accountable to the Vice President of Customer Relations, Branch Stuckey. He's known as a calm, reasonable man who nevertheless keeps the pressure steady—if his memos or phone calls are not answered within a reasonable amount of time, he is sure to pay a personal visit to ask why. Both he and you share the vision of the technical writing department as the most important medium through which customers receive information about Interaxion's products and services.

You and your staff are responsible for writing the promotional materials and specifications that anchor every service's marketing campaign, and for writing easy-to-follow manuals for their use. You're also accountable for maintaining and updating the Interaxion Web site.

You and Stuckey have jointly decided that the clientele would be well-served by two additional projects. The first, a general technical glossary, is to be available both in print and from Interaxion's Web site, and will help customers to understand the increasingly complex jargon involved in implementing the company's services. You and Stuckey have set a deadline of six months for the launch of this glossary.

Another document you've decided will be helpful is a Frequently Asked Questions (FAQ)/Troubleshooting guide for each of the company's line of services. This will require close collaboration with both the Technical Support and Communications departments. This a project that is of particular interest to the president, who wants a progress report submitted at the end of each month.

As a matter of principle, you try to work no more than a standard 8-to-5 workday. The three-day focus for this exercise is the Monday-Wednesday span of the 23rd through the 25th. The items you find in your in-box are items 1 through 10 and a general information folder compiled by your trusted assistant, Fred. On Tuesday afternoon, a meeting is scheduled from 2 p.m. to 4. p.m. that will include the marketing staff and your department, to discuss reasons why the marketing campaign for Interaxion's security services is not doing well. Tina Niu, Vice President of Marketing, seems to believe it's because the promotional material is too technical and jargony. You met briefly with your staff on Friday to prepare a response to this, but were unsatisfied with the results. You'd like at least another two hours with your writers before meeting with the marketing department.

On the following pages are a list of important departments and personnel at Interaxion, a to-do list, messages, memos, and a planner covering the three-day period. Read the instructions below, then assume you have just arrived Monday morning to find these items in your in-basket.

1. *Look over the list of officers, the planner, the to-do list, and in-basket items quickly, to get an idea of the tasks to be done.*

2. *In the spaces provided in the left margin of the to-do list, indicate the priority of each item, and note how you would dispose of each. Priorities should be labeled in the following manner:*

    AB priorities = those that are both important and urgent
    A priorities = those that are important, but not particularly urgent (can be deferred)
    B priorities = those that are urgent, but not so important
    X priorities = neither urgent nor important

3. *After reading the in-basket items, do the following:*

    a. *First, decide which items can be delegated, and to whom. Use Form B, Delegated Calls and Correspondence, to list and prioritize these items.*
    b. *Next, prioritize the items to which you must respond personally on Form C, Personal Calls and Correspondence.*

4. *Take the planning guide and schedule the tasks you have in front of you. Be sure to allow some "flexible time" to handle any interruptions or crises.*

Interaxion

Important Departments/Personnel:

<u>President/CEO</u>: Marlane Liddell
    <u>VP Marketing</u>: Tina Niu
      Marketing Director: Brian Paulsen
      General Sales Manager: Maxine Patton
    <u>VP Service Delivery</u>: Owen Stark
      Director of Engineering: Anna Karpov
      Chief Information Architect: Juan Machuca
        (Various Project Managers)
    <u>VP Finance</u>: Tom Wilson
      Treasurer: Mary Stravinsky
      Comptroller: Barbara Bernstein
        John Slingsby, Director of Cost Analysis
        Ruth Nielsen, Director of Budgeting and Accounting
    <u>VP Administration and Human Resources</u>: Tariq Nayim
      Director of Human Resources: Amos Otis
      Director of Administration: Nancy Frank
    <u>VP Customer Relations</u>: Branch Stuckey
      Director of Communications: Alvin Gehring
      Director of Technical Support: Hollis Holt
      Chief Technical Writer: T. SMITH
        Terry Appleton, Technical Writer
        Samir Naramayan, Technical Writer/Web Designer
        Jim Mason, Technical Writer
        Tracy Livingston, Associate Writer
          Fred Cummings, Assistant to **T. SMITH**
          Stacia Cocker, Office Assistant

Things to Do:

_____   •attend meeting on downtime of hosting service. Some clients have fallen below the promised 99.999% uptime, and the company needs to devise ways to improve performance.

Disposition: _____

_____

_____

_____   •meet with technical writing staff for input on the promotion of security services.

Disposition: _____

_____

_____

_____   •meet with staff to outline promotional copy for download hosting service — now looks as if it will be rolled out in about 8 months.

Disposition: _____

_____

_____

_____   •see what's up with Mason's overtime.

Disposition: _____

_____

_____

Things to Do (cont'd):

_____ •contact people who sent in resumes for associate writing job--Sanchez looked best of all, but I'll interview Larkin, too. Reject Yancey and Crespin.

Disposition: _____

_____

_____

_____ •meet with writers to assign updates to manuals for each of the security services. Should take about an hour.

Disposition: _____

_____

_____

_____ •check on the progress of the technical glossary--Mason is falling way, way behind.

Disposition: _____

_____

_____

_____ •check with human resources and budgeting to ask about availability for part-time position, to compile the FAQ/Troubleshooting guide—even with new associate, not enough staff time to devote to this.

Disposition: _____

_____

_____

_____ •proofread/line-edit customer manual (8 hours work at least) for storage network operation, and send it to the printer. Must be done by you personally, and by Thursday morning! Several customers have already purchased network and are waiting.

Disposition: _____

_____

NOTE TO: _T. SMITH_____

DATE _20th_____ TIME _4:50 p.m._

WHILE YOU WERE OUT

M _Janet Yancey_____

OF _____

PHONE _(_____)_____
       AREA CODE   NUMBER   EXTENSION

	Telephoned	✓	Please Call
	Called to See You		Will Call Again
	Wants to See You		Returned Your Call

Message _Anxious to speak w/you about_
associate writer position.

Item 2

Memorandum

To: T. SMITH
CC: Hollis Holt, Director of Technical Support
From: Alvin Gehring, Director of Communications
Date: 20th
Re: Web site e-mail service

I've been contacted a few times in the past couple of weeks by customers who have visited our Web site and wanted to e-mail us a question. Apparently some of them have clicked on the "e-mail us" hypertext button from a product description page, and nothing has happened.

I know that this is probably a very small-scale problem, and that the more persistent customers will know to simply e-mail us using their own mail programs. But I can't help thinking we might be losing some potential customers without this direct link.

Can you look into this and see what the problem is? I'd like to find out as soon as possible.

Memorandum

To: T. SMITH
CC:
From: Marlane Liddell, CEO and President
Date: 23rd
Re: Updates on troubleshooting guide and arrangement with Sturdevant

---

Just a note to remind you that I'll want to meet with you soon to talk about progress on the FAQ/Troubleshooting Guide.

I've also recently received a letter from Sturdevant Publishing about our arrangement with them. Their $6500 payment is figured into our revenues for the quarter, so we'll need to meet that contract deadline.

Let me know when you're available to meet—and when we do meet, make sure you're ready with the good news.

NOTE TO: __T. SMITH__

DATE __23rd__   TIME __9:00 am__

WHILE YOU WERE OUT

M __Philip Larkin__

OF _____

PHONE (____) _____ _____
     AREA CODE   NUMBER   EXTENSION

✓	Telephoned		Please Call
	Called to See You		Will Call Again
	Wants to See You		Returned Your Call

Message __Wants to know your decision about associate writer position.__

Memorandum

To: T. SMITH
CC: Terry Appleton, Samir Naramayan, Jim Mason, Technical Writers
From: Tracy Livingston, Associate Writer
Date: 23rd
Re: Security services/marketing

I hope this doesn't sound too compulsive, but I know we all worked very hard on the specs and promotional materials for security services, and I can't accept the idea that people aren't buying in because they don't understand our copy.

I conducted a little of my own market research over the weekend—interviewing purchasers from about a dozen clients who've bought other services from us, but went with another company for security. There were a few different reasons, but many clients seem to have placed the blame on some questionable architecture.

When pressed, a few said that they did find some parts of the promotional copy a little hard to follow—but added that it wasn't the factor that affected our buying decision.

We'll need to be careful about how we present this, so it doesn't appear we're shifting blame to Service Delivery. This can be one of the things we decide together when we meet (when are we meeting again? Isn't the meeting with Marketing tomorrow afternoon?).

Before we do meet, I hope you'll all take a look at some of the results of the interviews, enclosed here. It should take about a half-hour to get through them.

Item 6

NOTE TO: _T. SMITH_

DATE _23rd_ _____ TIME _8:24 a.m._

WHILE YOU WERE OUT

M _Jim Mason_

OF _____

PHONE (____) _____ _____
     AREA CODE   NUMBER   EXTENSION

✔	Telephoned		Please Call
	Called to See You		Will Call Again
	Wants to See You		Returned Your Call

Message _Will come in at 10:30 a.m. today — had to take his wife to a rescheduled hospital appointment. Says he's sorry — the only time he could do it._

Memorandum

To: All Department Heads
CC:
From: Marlane Liddell, President and CEO
Date: 23rd
Re: Meeting on hosting service downtime

A reminder: our meeting on resolving the hosting service downtime problem will be this Wednesday, the 25th, from 1 p.m. to 4 p.m.

Enclosed is a short examination of issues, compiled by Alvin Gehring Hollis Holt, and Owen Stark, that will need to be addressed if we are to improve the uptime of our Web hosting service. This is probably the most important problem facing our company today, and we'll all need to work together to resolve it as soon as possible.

Please take a look through the enclosed 30 pages to get an idea of what's holding us back, and try to have some ideas for resolution ready by the time we meet Wednesday.

Item 8

2642 Avenue of the Americas

New York, NY 00000

Sturdevant Publishing

November 10

T. SMITH
Chief Technical Writer
Interaxion
3445 Newton Ave.
Cambridge, MA 00000

Dear T. SMITH:

We at Sturdevant are pleased you've decided to contribute to our forthcoming publication, *The Encyclopedia of Technical Publishing*, to be compiled over the next 9 months and released early next year.

Last month, you agreed to send us a general profile of your company and a specific description of the different forms of writing (manuals, proposals, letters, specifications, etc.) performed by your department, along with a few recent samples of your work.

As you know, payment of $6500 to Interaxion was contingent on the delivery of this information by the end of the current month. We expect that you have every intention of honoring this contract, but we haven't heard from you recently and wanted to extend a reminder to you in any case.

Sincerely,

Bob Francis

Editorial Director

Memorandum

To:　　T. SMITH
CC:　　Jim Mason, Technical Writer; Barbara Bernstein, Comptroller
From:　Ruth Nielsen, Director of Budgeting and Accounting
Date:　23rd
Re:　　Overtime

Our records show an unusual amount of overtime charged to the company by your department over the last month. In order to meet our budget targets for the quarter, you'll need to work with your employees to reduce the number of hours they work each week.

If you're unable to reduce these hours, it may be necessary to conduct an internal audit in order to verify their necessity. Of course this is simply adding time and expenditure to the situation, and we'd like to avoid it entirely.

Please let us know how this situation is resolved.

NOTE TO: **T. SMITH**

DATE **23rd**   TIME **7:50 a.m.**

WHILE YOU WERE OUT

M **Janet Yancey**

OF _____

PHONE (_____) _____ _____
     AREA CODE   NUMBER   EXTENSION

	Telephoned	✓	Please Call
	Called to See You	✓	Will Call Again
	Wants to See You		Returned Your Call

Message **Wants to speak w/ you ASAP about associate writer position — will keep calling.**

General Information Folder:

1. Additional interdepartmental memos—about a dozen of them. Don't need a response but should be read for information. Should take about a half hour.

2. Eight news and trade newspapers and magazines—about two hours' worth of reading.

3. About 20 items of junk mail—should be reviewed. Will take about 30 minutes.

4. A detailed report—in addition to Liddell's 30-page report and Livingston's interviews—that need to be studied for possible action. It's a compilation of customer-satisfaction ratings for the company's other services, including their ratings of the documentation for each on a broad range of criteria, including readability, ease of understanding, and thoroughness. This should require about an hour.

DELEGATED CALLS AND CORRESPONDENCE

Priority	*Item*	*Delegated to:*
_____		
_____		
_____		
_____		
_____		
_____		
_____		
_____		
_____		

PERSONAL CALLS AND CORRESPONDENCE.

Priority   *Item*   *Response:*

_____

_____

_____

_____

_____

_____

_____

_____

_____

Priority   *Item*   *Response:*

	23 Monday	24 Tuesday	25 Wednesday
7 AM			
8			
9			
10			
11			
12 PM			
1			
2			
3			
4			
5			
6 PM			
7			

KEY (CORRECT ANSWERS)

Discussion of Inbox Examination #1:

Senior Technical Writer/Content Director, Interaxion

One of the first things you should realize, when looking over all the information in front of you, is that there won't be enough time within the next three days for you to do the things on your list, as well as the tasks required by your in-box items. This is hardly surprising for a senior worker at a mid-sized company, but you'll have to decide quickly what can be either eliminated from your schedule, or postponed.

To-Do List:

In this case, the prime candidate for elimination is the three-hour meeting on the downtime of the company's hosting service. While the president is anxious about it, and wants input from people from all departments, there's really not much a technical writing staff can do about the problem. You should try to free up these three hours—speaking with the president personally and explaining what needs to be done by you and your staff in the next three days, and offering to send a representative to the meeting who will report back to you.

As chief technical writer, there are two situations that are both important and urgent: your meeting with marketing department to discuss the quality of your staff's promotional materials, and the huge task of editing the manual for Interaxion's storage network users. Since some customers have already purchased the network, they'll need the manual as soon as possible. The meeting with Marketing is on Tuesday, and you have two tasks to complete before then: read through the information supplied by Tracy Livingston, and call the afternoon meeting with the writers on Monday—they'll need to drop everything in the afternoon for this.

Once the most important and urgent items are taken care of, you should turn your attention to tasks that are important, but not as pressing. You'll need to meet with the staff for two further purposes: outlining promotional copy for the company's downloading hosting service (not that urgent, since the rollout isn't for another 8 months), and assigning updates for the manuals for security service users. Since your copy on the promotional materials for these services is being questioned by the marketing department, it's probably best to schedule this meeting after you've met with Marketing and these questions have been resolved. You'll also need to see if you can find a way to hire part-time help for compiling the FAQ/Troubleshooting guide, since this is of extreme importance to the president.

Urgent matters that aren't quite as significant as the others facing you right now are the progress of the technical glossary—not due out for another six months—and the related problem of Jim Mason's excessive overtime. His memo about taking his wife to the hospital hints that he might be going through some personal problems, and if they're affecting his work, this situation needs to be resolved soon.

Discussion (cont'd)

Delegated Calls and Correspondence:

Janet Yancey may insist on speaking with you personally, but it may simply be that she wants a yes or no answer regarding her hiring. For now, it should be enough to have your assistant send her a letter. Assuming Fred is informed about the progress of your arrangements with Sturdevant—and assuming the contract is being honored—he can also send a reply to them. The e-mail problem, presented in the memo from Hollis Holt, is best left to the expertise of your Web designer, Samir Naramayan.

Personal Calls and Correspondence:

It appears that the news on the progress of the FAQ/Troubleshooting guide is not that good, but you'll need to set up a meeting with the president anyway to tell her so. It might be a good time to state your case about needing more help. You should send a memo to set a meeting time, and to reassure her about the arrangement with Sturdevant.

Since you do intend to interview Philip Larkin about the associate writer position, you should probably call him personally to set this up—though some managers might leave this to an assistant. It's acceptable to include this in the "delegated" column as well.

The memo from the president is simply a re-statement of your obligation to attend the hosting service downtime meeting—and you've determined you can't do this. You should make every attempt to speak with the president personally, to explain why, and to see if sending your assistant is acceptable. You should also give the 30-page report to your assistant, Fred, to have him either outline it for you or see if any of it is relevant to the technical writing staff at all.

Jim Mason appears to be in some trouble, and he may need your help to resolve it—especially since his problems are being noticed by the budgeting department. Since it would be best to discuss it privately, out of the office, you might meet him somewhere for lunch and try to work things out. He'll have to find a way to get things done within a regular 40-hour week.

Planner:

Filling in the planner can be done in a number of ways—as long as everything on your to-do list and in your inbox gets taken care of, and in an appropriate sequence. The most difficult thing to schedule will probably be the meeting with the writers about promotional copy for the security services. It's a short-notice meeting, for one thing, and you'll need to look over Livingston's interviews first. The meeting must happen before the Tuesday meeting with marketing—and Since Jim Mason won't be in until 10:30 on Monday, it will have to take place after that. The tight window requires that the meeting happen Monday afternoon or Tuesday morning. Items such as progress on other projects can be discussed briefly, toward the end of scheduled meetings.

In addition, it wouldn't make sense to schedule the other meeting—regarding the updates to existing security service manuals—until after some of the questions raised by both the marketing department and Livingston's interviews have been resolved. This will have to take place some time on Wednesday.

Things to Do: 22

Priority	_Item_

_____X_____ •attend meeting on downtime of hosting service. Some clients have fallen below the promised 99.999% uptime, and the company needs to devise ways to improve performance.

Disposition: _____Contact Marlane Liddell personally to explain why you can't_

make the meeting. Ask if you can send an assistant to take notes, promise to

review them later and get back to her with ideas.

_____AB_____ •meet with technical writing staff for input on the promotion of security services.

Disposition: _____Schedule meeting for Monday, the 23rd, after Mason gets in._

_____A_____ •meet with staff to outline promotional copy for download hosting service —now looks as if it will be rolled out in about 8 months.

Disposition: _____Schedule after more urgent meetings—maybe combine_

with manual update meeting.

_____B_____ •see what's up with Mason's overtime.

Disposition: _____Meet with him soon and privately, away from other_

writers.

_____A_____ •contact people who sent in resumes for associate writing job--Sanchez looked best of all, but I'll interview Larkin, too. Reject Yancey and Crespin.

Disposition: _____Have Fred send letter to Yancey and Crespin; call Larkin and_

Sanchez personally to set up interviews

Things to Do (cont'd):

_____A_____ •meet with writers to assign updates to manuals for each of the security services. Should take about an hour.

Disposition: <u>*Schedule meeting after all other concerns regarding security*</u>

<u>*services documentation have been cleared up—no sooner than Wednesday.*</u>

_____B_____ •check on the progress of the technical glossary--Mason is falling way, way behind.

Disposition: <u>*A quick check that can be slipped in at the end of another*</u>

<u>*meeting—try for Monday or Wednesday.*</u>

_____A_____ •check with human resources and budgeting to ask about availability for part-time position, to compile the FAQ/Troubleshooting guide—even with new associate, not enough staff time to devote to this.

Disposition: <u>*Contact them personally, during flex time, before scheduling*</u>

<u>*meeting with Marlane Liddell.*</u>

_____AB_____ •proofread/line-edit customer manual (8 hours work at least) for storage network operation, and send it to the printer. Must be done by you personally, and by Thursday morning! Several customers have already purchased network and are waiting.

Disposition: <u>*Try to fit in big time blocks to devote to this—give it your*</u>

<u>*full attention.*</u>

DELEGATED CALLS AND CORRESPONDENCE

Priority	Item	Delegated to:
X	#1—Yancey call	Fred
A	#2—Holt memo	Samir
X	#8—Sturdevant letter	Fred will write response
X	#10—Yancey call	Fred
_____		
_____		
_____		
_____		

Priority	Item	Delegated to:

PERSONAL CALLS AND CORRESPONDENCE

Priority	Item	Response:
A	#3—Liddell memo	Brief memo
A	#4—Larkin call	Phone call for interview
AB	#7—Liddell memo	Personal visit
A	#9—Nielsen memo	Meet w/ Mason and write memo

	23 Monday	24 Tuesday	25 Wednesday
7 AM			
8	flex-time: delegate, make calls, set up meeting	flex-time: reading, sorting work on storage network manual	read customer sat. report
9	reading: interdept. memos, trade publications		flex-time: schedule interviews
10			work on storage network manual
11			
12 PM		lunch, meeting w/ Mason	
1	flex-time: examine Livingston interviews	flex-time: sort through junk mail	meeting w. writers:
2	meeting w. writers:	meeting w/ Marketing	•assign updates to manuals, •outline download promo copy
3	•ideas for response to market-ing,		work on storage network manual
4	•progress of tech. glossary,	work on storage network manual	
5	•FAQ/Troubleshooting guide		
6 PM			
7			

EXAMINATION SECTION

IN-BASKET

Senior Graphic Designer, Callens New Media

You are B. GARCIA, the senior graphic designer of Callens New Media, a small publisher of materials (newsletters, meeting planners, city guides, and more) for those who organize and attend trade conventions. You have a background both in art and in computer technology, and because the company is small, you play a dual role as both a project manager for the publications and a troubleshooter/technical support resource when there are problems with the publishing software or the company Web site, which you designed and now maintain.

Because of your company's size, its success has relied primarily on occupying this smaller niche in the business publishing market. Your boss, Reynold Callens, would like to draw upon your technological knowledge and expand services to include Web design and servicing, and eventually to include such things as hosting and downloading services for professional associations who conduct merchandising operations from their Web sites. In your last evaluation, you and your boss set an objective to produce a Web-based demonstration of the services that will be available to anyone who visits the company Web site. The deadline for completion of this project has been left open, but your boss is pressing you to show him results soon.

The organizational structure of the company is somewhat loose, due to its size, and could use some readjustment. There are no vice presidents; simply a few team leaders, each overseeing a few workers. Though each team leader reports directly to Reynold Callens, you are often approached by people from other departments for input on solutions, because you were one of the company's first employees and have more knowledge about clients and products, as well as some working knowledge of the earlier and simpler versions of the company's computer networks. Though you don't resent being thought of as a "catch-all" for projects or problems that don't fit neatly into the company's departmental structure, you believe your own responsibilities are keeping you busy enough. The added pressures from other departments is getting stressful for both you and your staff, whom you sense are becoming slightly indignant at the repeated encroachments on their time.

You and your staff bear much responsibility for the timeliness and completeness of the company's current operations. Your responsibilities include making sure the publications are proofread and camera-ready, making arrangements with the printers, arranging for distribution of your company's products to individual conferees, and offering the final say for photos, illustrations, or maps in every publication. Traditionally, you have been the one who communicates with customers directly about certain projects, answering questions or addressing concerns—though these are tasks which should logically fall to your production assistant, Craig Long.

The company's size also means that you have no office assistant. Any calls that come in are handled either by you or your staff of three—your associate graphic artist, Sally

Montrose, your technical writer/content provider, Stan Lee, or your production assistant, Craig Long. You hired all three of them, and you're generally pleased with their work so far—though you admit to having a hard time delegating tasks that can be handled by one or more of them. This is due, you admit, to your own reluctance to surrender control of details, and not with any problem you have with their work thus far.

The three-day focus is the Monday-Wednesday span of the 16th through the 18th—a period that coincides with the beginning of a convention in Cincinnati, to which Craig Long has been dispatched to oversee the distribution of materials to individual participants on Monday and early Tuesday. The items you find in your in-box are items 1 through 10 and a general information folder that you have compiled yourself, which contains items that you believe will need your attention, sooner or later.

On Tuesday afternoon from 1 p.m. to 3 p.m., you are meeting with your boss and an outside consultant, both to check on the progress of the demonstration and to discuss the resources that will be needed to make the proposed Web services available to clients. You'll need to supply an idea of manpower and work-hour needs for different types of sites—and you'll need to get input from your staff to do this, which you estimate will take an hour. Since Craig Long is in Cincinnati, the meeting will have to be a conference call.

On Wednesday morning from 9 a.m. to 11 a.m. you are meeting one-one-one with Callens to more clearly define two things: First, what your own personal responsibilities are, now that the company is growing and your title of "graphic designer" doesn't seem to quite encompass all the managerial tasks you've been taking on. Second, the extent and limit of what your team members are expected to do. You will need to go to this meeting armed with four proposed job descriptions: for yourself, which you will need to write before the meeting (anticipated time: 2 hours), and for Montrose, Lee, and Long, who have already been assigned to write their own. You'll need to meet together with them for an hour, to go over their written descriptions, before you present them to the boss.

You and your staff like to work a normal eight-hour day whenever possible. The day begins at 8 and ends at 5, so an hour-long lunch is the custom, though because of the recent pressures at the workplace it's often much shorter than that.

On the following pages are a list of important departments and personnel at Callens New Media, a to-do list, messages, memos, and a planner covering the three-day period. Read the instructions below, then assume you have just arrived Monday morning to find these items in your in-basket.

1.   *Look over the list of officers, the planner, the to-do list, and in-basket items quickly, to get an idea of the tasks to be done.*

2.   *In the spaces provided in the left margin of the to-do list, indicate the priority of each item, and note how you would dispose of each. Priorities should be labeled in the following manner:*

AB priorities = those that are both important and urgent
A priorities = those that are important, but not particularly urgent (can be deferred)
B priorities = those that are urgent, but not so important
X priorities = neither urgent nor important

3.   *After reading the in-basket items, do the following:*

   a.   *First, decide which items can be delegated, and to whom. Use Form B, Delegated Calls and Correspondence, to list and prioritize these items.*
   b.   *Next, prioritize the items to which you must respond personally on Form C, Personal Calls and Correspondence.*

4.   *Take the planning guide and schedule the tasks you have in front of you. Be sure to allow some "flexible time" to handle any interruptions, crises, or new issues or correspondence.*

Callens New Media

Important Departments/Personnel:

<u>Owner/CEO</u>: Reynold Callens

<u>Marketing and Sales Team</u>:
> Marketing and Sales Director: Roland Brooks (team leader)
> Sales Region 1: Tom Spencer
> Sales Region 2: Lorna Stans

<u>Administrative Team</u>:
> Accounting Officer: Terry Spath (team leader)
> Budget and Accounting Assistant: Ed Stein
> Information Architect: Gordon Wayne
> Manager, Enterprise Systems: Frank Luntz
> Director of Human Resources: Monica Torres

<u>Production/Customer Relations Team</u>:
> **Senior Graphic Designer: B. Garcia (team leader)**
> Associate Graphic Artist: Sally Montrose
> Technical Writer/Content Provider: Stan Lee
> Production Assistant: Craig Long

Things to Do:

Priority   *Item*

_____   • check and respond to e-mails, especially any from clients, hotels, or
                    Craig Long in Cincinnati. Time required: half an hour

                    Disposition: _____

                    _____

                    _____

_____   •write job description for Wednesday meeting. Would like to have this
                    done before meeting with Callens on Tuesday, in order to be ready if there
                    is time. Two hours.

                    Disposition: _____

                    _____

                    _____

_____   •update the company Web site to add newly hired personnel, and to more
                    accurately reflect the company's products and services. Estimated time: 3
                    hours—one hour design and layout, one hour writing content, one hour
                    formatting/coding.

                    Disposition: _____

                    _____

                    _____

_____   •deliver proofs for newsletter to local printer, for next month's
                    radiologists' convention in Cleveland. Should take about a half hour.

                    Disposition: _____

                    _____

                    _____

Things to Do (cont'd):

_____ •respond to customer requests for information about upcoming projects and publications (requests for proofs, information about content, requests for edits, etc.). Should take about an hour and a half.

Disposition: _____

_____

_____

_____ •find illustrations, maps and photos for meeting planner, for next month's convention in Denver. Already been designed. Needs to be ready for printer within two weeks. Should take about two hours.

Disposition: _____

_____

_____

_____ • call temp agency, hotels to arrange for drops (hotel charges for doorman to make drops) for Philadelphia convention that begins this Thursday and runs through Sunday. Should take about an hour.

Disposition: _____

_____

_____

_____ •perform design and layout for a meeting planner and city guide for an upcoming convention in Nashville. Initial design must be done by you and should take about 8 hours total; you need to spend at least 3 hours on it before Thursday to stay on schedule.

Disposition: _____

_____

_____

General Information Folder:

1. Several articles in trade journals, flagged by Reynold Callens to be read by you and discussed with him at a later, unspecified date. Should take about an hour

2. About 30 items of junk mail—should be scanned. About an hour's worth of reading.

3. Additional interdepartmental memos—ten or so. Don't require a response but should be read for information. Should take about a half hour.

4. A written proposal from a software vendor detailing the newest features of the latest version of their desktop publishing suite. They are not your vendor but want you to switch to their line. You want to consider it. It's about an hour and a half of reading.

FORM B: DELEGATED CALLS AND CORRESPONDENCE

Priority	*Item*	*Delegated to:*
_____		
_____		
_____		
_____		
_____		
_____		
_____		
_____		

FORM C: PERSONAL CALLS AND CORRESPONDENCE

Priority   *Item*   *Response:*

_____

_____

_____

_____

_____

_____

_____

_____

_____

Item 1

From: smontrose@cnm.com
Date: June 15, 7:22:39 PM EST
Subject: Monday
To: clong@cnm.com, bgarcia@cnm.com

Wanted to let you both know in advance that I'll be leaving the office tomorrow (Monday), after lunch. My son is sick and has an appointment with the doctor in the afternoon. I haven't forgotten our meeting—I'll be back first thing Tuesday morning.

Item 2

Memorandum

To: All Team Leaders
CC:
From: Reynold
Date: June 14
Re: The Future

I've been thinking a lot over the past month about the direction this company is taking, and I think you're all right, to a degree: We've outgrown the informal structure that was in place when we first started. Roles aren't as clearly defined as they need to be, and there is some overlap in responsibilities. I realize the potential for conflict here, and I'm grateful that you've all been able to bear these growing pains so graciously. You'd tell me if you were having any problems with each other, right?

Anyway, I think it's time we sat down together and had a serious talk about the future of this company—how it is structured, what each of our roles is going to be, an d where we out to be investing our resources in the coming years. It's a serious subject that deserves your serious consideration. I'm tentatively scheduling a leadership meeting for 1-4 on Wednesday. If there's some reason why that won't work—I know the Philadelphia convention begins the next day, but I'm assuming we're on top of that—then let me know. Otherwise, bring your best ideas.

--Reynold

Item 3

NOTE TO: B. Garcia

DATE: Friday, June 13th   TIME: 7:00 pm

WHILE YOU WERE OUT

M: Horst, concierge

OF: Cincinnati Hampden Court Hotel

PHONE: (513)   888-7777   55
AREA CODE   NUMBER   EXTENSION

X	Telephoned		Please Call
	Called to See You		Will Call Again
	Wants to See You		Returned Your Call

Message: Materials haven't arrived yet for next week's convention - can't get hold of printer. Call back ASAP!

— Sally

Item 4

From: glesst@ana.org
Date: June 16, 8:07:12 AM EST
Subject: meeting
To: bgarcia@cnm.com

I have the advance proofs of the newsletter for our convention next month in Denver—thanks for sending them along so promptly. I have some questions. First, a general question about the style guide your staff uses (I'm curious about some of the choices you've made in indentation and layout—I think I might like a few changes to be made here). I also have a few corrections to make about the details of the convention and some of the bios that appear on the last page.

Thanks again—I hope I'll hear from you soon.

--Teresa Gless

Item 5

From: clong@cnm.com
Date: June 16, 8:07:12 AM EST
Subject: meeting
To: smontrose@cnm.com, bgarcia@cnm.com

I know we have to have a conference call today or tomorrow, but things are getting hairy here in Cincinnati and I'm going to need to stay on top of things nearly around the clock. I can be available today from 3-5 pm or tomorrow from 8-9 in the morning. Give me a call on the cell at either of those two times.

I'll be back in the office no later than 3 p.m. on Tuesday. See you both then.

Item 6

1947 Nautilus Ct.
Mystic, CT 00000

June 8

Production Department
Callens New Media
7875 Shore Drive
Tampa, FL 00000

To Whom it May Concern:

I'm a Printing Technology Professional with many years of experience in the printing trade. As you will see from my attached resume, I have a plethora of skills which are directly related to the mission of a printing or marketing firm.

My skills in printing, graphic arts, web site design and customer service would be an excellent fit with any company utilizing the printing arts.

With over 12 years in commercial printing and 20 years of involvement with computers, it is my hope that your company could use a person with my expertise.

I am a very positive individual with excellent people skills and have previously been an inspiring force in team situations.

I'd like a chance to convince you that my skills and energy would be an asset to your firm. If needed, I can also provide a comprehensive portfolio that exhibits my greatest accomplishments in the last 10 years of my career, as well as letters of recommendation from previous employers.

Sincerely,

Fred G. Moose

Item 7

NOTE TO: B. Garcia

DATE Friday, June 13th   TIME 9:00 a.m.

WHILE YOU WERE OUT

MS. Vivian Wu

OF Hood Printing, Oregon

PHONE (503) 555-2424
AREA CODE   NUMBER   EXTENSION

✗	Telephoned		Please Call
	Called to See You		Will Call Again
	Wants to See You		Returned Your Call

Message Questions about sizing, res of photos for DHA convention in Portland next week, (25th?)

— Lorna

Item 8

NOTE TO: B. Garcia

DATE Monday, June 16th   TIME 8:11 am

WHILE YOU WERE OUT

MS Merman

OF National League of Dental Hygienists

PHONE (212)   777-1234   203
      AREA CODE   NUMBER   EXTENSION

X	Telephoned		Please Call
	Called to See You		Will Call Again
	Wants to See You		Returned Your Call

Message Doesn't have confirmation that materials have arrived at hotel and are ready for distribution at Philadelphia Convention. Begins on Thurs., 19th.

—Sally

Item 9

Memorandum

To: B. GARCIA
CC: Reynold Callens, President
From: Roland Brooks, Director of Marketing and Sales
Date: June 13
Re: Marketing our new services

B.:

I'm going to be meeting with our sales staff next week about how to begin planting the seeds of interest in our new Web services to our clients—especially the national medical groups. The problem is, I'm not yet very knowledgeable about what these services are going to be and how, exactly, they are going to serve our clients. I'll be grateful if I could be brought up to speed on the technical details, but most especially I'll be interested in being able to explain, in layman's terms, what each of these proposed services is going to enable our clients to do.

Would it be possible to meet for an hour or so this week to talk about this? Thanks in advance.

Item 10

NOTE TO: B. Garcia

DATE: Monday, June 16th   TIME: 7:45 am

WHILE YOU WERE OUT

M: Horst, concierge

OF: Cincinnati Hampden Court Hotel

PHONE: (513) 888-7777 55
  AREA CODE   NUMBER   EXTENSION

X	Telephoned		Please Call
	Called to See You		Will Call Again
	Wants to See You		Returned Your Call

Message: Materials are there at front desk, but hasn't heard from anyone at CNM about distribution. Conferees calling to ask about it. Not his job! Call back ASAP!

— Sally

20

	16 Monday	17 Tuesday	18 Wednesday
7			
8			
9			
10			
11			
12			
1			
2			
3			
4			
5			
6			

	16 Monday	17 Tuesday	18 Wednesday
7			

KEY (CORRECT ANSWERS)

Discussion of Inbox Examination

Senior Graphic Designer, Callens New Media

There are 24 total work hours in these three days, and the four meetings listed in the introduction—with your staff, to discuss the requirements of the Web services demonstration; with Reynold Callens and the consultant; with the staff to go over job descriptions; and with Callens again—consume six of these hours, leaving you with 18 hours in which to handle everything else. It's not enough time—and so it's time for you to do what you've been reluctant to do so far: delegate.

To-Do List:

Since the convention in Cincinnati begins on the 16th, you should check your e-mails to see if any are concerned with it—and it turns out a couple of them are. This task should be done before any others, so that you can perform the necessary follow-up.

There are two other tasks on the To-Do List that are both important and urgent: the second (writing your job description, which you'd like to have ready in case Callens is ready to discuss it at Tuesday's meeting) and the seventh (arranging the details for the Philadelphia convention). The job description should be done as soon as possible on Monday. Ordinarily, the details of the Philadelphia convention should be delegated to Craig Long, your production assistant, but since the convention begins Thursday, and he won't return until Tuesday afternoon, you'd be better off taking care of it yourself, and soon.

There are several possibilities for delegation on the list. The third item—updating the company Web site—is a team effort that should involve all members. Design and layout should be Montrose's input, and it's Lee's job to write the content. Long can help them when he returns. Since you are the most technically proficient, you can handle the formatting and coding. You don't have three hours to spend on this—your commitment should not exceed one hour.

The fifth task—responding to customer requests—is specifically mentioned in the introduction as the kind of job you should be turning over to your production assistant, Craig Long. This isn't urgent and can be done by him when he returns from Cincinnati.

Another task that should be delegated to Lee or Montrose, or both, is the sixth item: finding graphic content for the Denver planner. It is a job well within their responsibilities.

The fourth task, delivering the Cleveland proofs, could be delegated to Long when he returns, but it's not a time-consuming job—it could probably be done on the way home from work, if you leave a little early.

The last task—three hours of design and layout for Nashville—is all yours. You will need to fit in your three hours somewhere during these three days.

Discussion (cont'd)

Delegated Calls and Correspondence:

Item 4, Teresa Gless's inquiry about the Denver materials' content, is best left to the person who wrote it. We can assume that was Stan Lee. Similarly, item 7 is a question about illustrations, and so should go to Sally Montrose.

It shouldn't be your job at all to answer an unsolicited letter of application to employment in your department. You should send item 6 straight to Monica Torres, human resources director.

You can admire Roland Brooks' enthusiasm for promoting the new Web services, but it should be obvious to anyone that the company hasn't even made the final decision about what these services will be. Instead of a one-on-one meeting with him, you should invite him to Tuesday's discussion with the consultant, or talk about it over lunch.

Personal Calls and Correspondence:

Nearly all of the in-box items that should be handled personally are both important and urgent. Items 1 and 5—emails from Long and Montrose about their availability for the conference call—simply require the quick response that the only possible time for the conference call about the work requirements for the demonstration is 8-9 Tuesday morning. You should remember this when filling out your planner.

Items 3 and 10 are your most urgent—the convention in Cincinnati is under way and the conferees don't have their newsletters or meeting planners yet. You need to get in touch with Long or the printer in Cincinnati to work this out immediately.

Item 8 presents a similar situation. Ordinarily, you should consider having Craig Long look into this, but since the convention begins Thursday, you probably ought to just take care of it.

The trickiest item, 2, takes a huge and unexpected chunk of important time away from your work this week. It's tricky because it's a memo from your boss, who should understand the irony of calling a meeting to eliminate role conflict and redundancies in the company—three hours after he has scheduled a one-on-one meeting with you to do basically the same thing.

You don't really have three hours to give for this meeting. You should suggest that most of your input on this issue will be presented during Wednesday's morning meeting, and that you'll still attend in the afternoon if he requires it—but you have a lot of work to do to keep things running smoothly. When filling out your planner, tentatively schedule things for 1-4 Wednesday that can, if needed, be put off.

Discussion (cont'd)

Planner:

There are many ways to fill out the planner, as long as the items on the to-do list and in your in-box are taken care of, and in a sequence that works. Fill in your four required meetings first. Here are some points to consider:

Montrose is out for Monday afternoon, which leaves only 8-9 Tuesday morning (the only other time Craig Long is available) for the staff conference call on the work requirements for the Web services demonstration.

You want your job description ready before Tuesday's meeting with Callens, in case he asks about it. Because you only have two hours total left to you on Tuesday morning, you should probably schedule this task for some time Monday.

Montrose is out Monday afternoon, and there are no meetings scheduled. This is a good time to work on the design and layout for the Nashville materials.

Flex-time is best scheduled at the margins of meetings, in case they begin early or run long.

As mentioned previously, you should try to convince Callens that your attendance at both Wednesday meetings is superfluous. Assume that he'll agree with you, but schedule tasks that can be postponed in case he insists.

Your input on the Web site updates—formatting and coding the changes made by your staff—should be done after you've given them a chance to provide the design and content. Try to schedule your work as late as possible during this time frame.

Things to Do:

Priority	_Item_

_____A_____ • check and respond to e-mails, especially any from clients, hotels, or Craig Long in Cincinnati. Time required: half an hour

Disposition: _Do this first, to head off any potential troubles in_

Cincinnati

_____AB_____ •write job description for Wednesday meeting. Would like to have this done before meeting with Callens on Tuesday, in order to be ready if there is time. Two hours.

Disposition: _Given the way time is shaping up, this should be done some_

time Monday.

_____A_____ •update the company Web site to add newly hired personnel, and to more accurately reflect the company's products and services. Estimated time: 3 hours—one hour design and layout, one hour writing content, one hour formatting/coding.

Disposition: _Take responsibility for formatting and coding, and delegate_

the rest to those who can do the work. Plan to spend an hour on it.

_____A_____ •deliver proofs for newsletter to local printer, for next month's radiologists' convention in Cleveland. Should take about a half hour.

Disposition: If you can make time, do this toward the end of one of your

work days. If not, have Long do it.

Things to Do (cont'd):

_____B_____   •respond to customer requests for information about upcoming projects and publications (requests for proofs, information about content, requests for edits, etc.). Should take about an hour and a half.

Disposition: Delegate this to Craig Long—it's why you hired him.

_____A_____   •Find illustrations, maps and photos for meeting planner, for next month's convention in Denver. Already been designed. Needs to be ready for printer within two weeks. Should take about two hours.

Disposition: Have your staff handle this—Lee and Montrose, or both.

_____AB_____   • call temp agency, hotels to arrange for drops (hotel charges for doorman to make drops) for Philadelphia convention that begins this Thursday and runs through Sunday. Should take about an hour.

Disposition: Since the convention is Thursday, and this has been your job

in the past, you should simply handle this as soon as you can.

_____B_____   •perform design and layout for a meeting planner and city guide for an upcoming convention in Nashville. Initial design must be done by you and should take about 8 hours total; you need to spend at least 3 hours on it before Thursday to stay on schedule.

Disposition: Try to find a long interrupted period of time to do this

work.

DELEGATED CALLS AND CORRESPONDENCE

Priority	Item	Delegated to:
A	4—Gless e-mail	Lee
X	6—Applicant cover letter	Torres
A	7—Hood Printing call	Montrose
X	9—Brooks memo	Callens, or lunch meeting

PERSONAL CALLS AND CORRESPONDENCE

Priority	Item	Response:
_AB_	1—Montrose e-mail	Brief reply: schedule conference call for 8-9 Tues. morning
_A_	2—Callens memo	Discuss w/him—try to cover this in Wed. morning meeting
_AB_	3—Cincinnati hotel call	Try to reach Long or the printer immediately
_AB_	5—Long e-mail	Brief reply: schedule conference call for 8-9 Tues. morning
_AB_	8—NLDH call	Check with the hotel and/or printer, then reply
_AB_	10—Cincinnati hotel call	Call Long or the printer immediately
_____		
_____		

	16 Monday	17 Tuesday	18 Wednesday
7			
8	flex-time: Cincinnati mess	demo meeting with staff	flex-time
	check additional e-mails		"
9	write job description for	flex-time	Callens meeting about job
	Tues. meeting	"	definitions
10	"	call temp. agencies, hotels,	"
	"	etc. for Philadelphia	"
11	read trade journal articles	scan junk mail	flex-time
	for Callens	"	"
12	lunch	lunch w/Brooks	lunch
	"		
1	design and layout, Nash-	demo meeting w/Callens,	respond to customer inqui-
	ville	consultant	ries (or delegate to Long)
2	"	"	"
	"	"	read software proposal
3	"	flex-time	"
	"	"	"
4	read dept. memos	job descriptions meeting	format and code Web site
	deliver Cleveland proofs	w/staff	updates
5			
6			
7			

SUPERVISION, ADMINISTRATION, MANAGEMENT AND ORGANIZATION
EXAMINATION SECTION

DIRECTIONS FOR THIS SECTION:
  Each question or incomplete statement is followed by several suggested answers or completions. Select the one that BEST answers the question or completes the statement. *PRINT THE LETTER OF THE CORRECT ANSWER IN THE SPACE AT THE RIGHT.*

TEST 1

1. In coaching a subordinate on the nature of decision-making,   1. ...
   an executive would be right if he stated that the one of the
   following which is *generally* the BEST definition of decision-
   making is:
   A. Choosing between alternatives
   B. Making diagnoses of feasible ends
   C. Making diagnoses of feasible means
   D. Comparing alternatives
2. Of the following, which one would be LEAST valid as a purpose 2. ...
   of an organizational policy statement? To
   A. keep personnel from performing improper actions and func-
      tions on routine matters
   B. prevent the mishandling of non-routine matters
   C. provide management personnel with a tool that precludes
      the need for their use of judgment
   D. provide standard decisions and approaches in handling
      problems of a recurrent nature
3. Much has been written criticizing bureaucratic organizations. 3. ...
   Current thinking on the subject is GENERALLY that
   A. bureaucracy is on the way out
   B. bureaucracy, though not perfect, is unlikely to be re-
      placed
   C. bureaucratic organizations are most effective in dealing
      with constant change
   D. bureaucratic organizations are most effective when deal-
      ing with sophisticated customers or clients
4. The development of alternate plans as a major step in plan-   4. ...
   ning will normally result in the planner having several possi-
   ble courses of action available. GENERALLY, this is
   A. *desirable,* since such development helps to determine the
      most suitable alternative and to provide for the unexpected
   B. *desirable,* since such development makes the use of planning
      premises and constraints unnecessary
   C. *undesirable,* since the planners should formulate only one
      way of achieving given goals at a given time
   D. *undesirable,* since such action restricts efforts to modify
      the planning to take advantage of opportunities
5. The technique of departmentation by task force includes the   5. ...
   assigning of a team or task force to a definite project or
   block of work which extends from the beginning to the completing of a wanted and definite type and quantity of work. Of the
   following, the MOST important factor aiding the successful use
   of this technique *normally* is
   A. having the task force relatively large, at least one
      hundred members
   B. having a definite project termination date established

   C. telling each task force member what his next assignment
      will be only after the current project ends
   D. utilizing it only for projects that are regularly re-
      curring

6. With respect to communication in small group settings such as 6. ...
   may occur in business, government and the military, it is GEN-
   ERALLY true that people *usually* derive more satisfaction and
   are usually more productive under conditions which
   A. permit communication only with superiors
   B. permit the minimum intragroup communication possible
   C. are generally restricted by management
   D. allow open communication among all group members

7. If an executive were asked to list some outstanding features   7. ...
   of decentralization, which one of the following would NOT be
   such a feature? Decentralization
   A. provides decision-making experience for lower level managers
   B. promotes uniformity of policy
   C. is a relatively new concept in management
   D. is similar to the belief in encouragement of free enterprise

8. Modern management experts have emphasized the importance of   8. ...
   the informal organization in motivating employees to increase
   productivity. Of the following, the characteristic which would
   have the MOST direct influence on employee motivation is the
   tendency of members of the informal organization to
   A. resist change   B. establish their own norms
   C. have similar outside interests
   D. set substantially higher goals than those of management

9. According to leading management experts, the decision-making   9. .
   process contains separate and distinct steps that must be ta-
   ken in an orderly sequence. Of the following arrangements,
   which one is in CORRECT order?
   A. I.Search for alternatives II.diagnosis III. comparison
      IV. choice
   B. I.Diagnosis II. comparison III. search for alternatives
      IV. choice
   C. I. Diagnosis II. search for alternatives III. comparison
      IV. choice
   D. I.Diagnosis II.search for alternatives III. choice IV.
      comparison

10. Of the following, the growth of professionalism in large or- 10. ...
    organizations can PRIMARILY be expected to result in
    A. greater equalization of power
    B. increased authoritarianism
    C. greater organizational disloyalty
    D. increased promotion opportunities

11. Assume an executive carries out his responsibilities to his 11. ...
    staff according to what is now known about managerial leader-
    ship. Which of the following statements would MOST accurately
    reflect his assumptions about proper management?
    A. Efficiency in operations results from allowing the human
       element to participate in a minimal way.
    B. Efficient operation results from balancing work considera-
       tions with personnel considerations.
    C. Efficient operation results from a workforce committed to
       its self interest.

D. Efficient operation results from staff relationships that produce a friendly work climate.

12. Assume that an executive is called upon to conduct a manage- 12. ...
ment audit. To do this properly, he would have to take certain
steps in a specific sequence. Of the following steps, which
step should this manager take FIRST?
A. Managerial performance must be surveyed.
B. A method of reporting must be established.
C. Management auditing procedures and documentation must be
developed.
D. Criteria for the audit must be considered.

13. If a manager is required to conduct a scientific investiga- 13. ...
tion of an organizational problem, the FIRST step he should
take is to
A. state his assumptions about the problem
B. carry out a search for background information
C. choose the right approach to investigate the validity
of his assumptions
D. define and state the problem

14. An executive would be *right* to assert that the principle of 14. ...
delegation states that decisions should be made PRIMARILY
A. by persons in an executive capacity qualified to make
them
B. by persons in a non-executive capacity
C. at as low an organization level of authority as practi-
cable
D. by the next lower level of authority

15. Of the following, which one is NOT regarded by management 15. ...
authorities as a FUNDAMENTAL characteristic of an *ideal* bu-
reaucracy?
A. Division of labor and specialization
B. An established hierarchy
C. Decentralization of authority
D. A set of operating rules and regulations

16. As the number of subordinates in a manager's span of control 16. ...
increases, the ACTUAL number of possible relationships
A. increases disproportionately to the number of subordinates
B. increases in equal number to the number of subordinates
C. reaches a stable level
D. will first increase then slowly decrease

17. An executive's approach to controlling the activities of his 17. ...
subordinates concentrated on ends rather than means, and was
diagnostic rather than punitive. This manager may MOST properly be characterized as using the managerial technique of
management-by-
A. exception   B. objectives   C. crisis   D. default

18. In conducting a training session on the administrative con- 18. ...
trol process, which of the following statements would be
LEAST valid for an executive to make? Controlling
A. requires checking upon assignments to see what is being
done
B. involves comparing what is being done to what ought to
be done
C. requires corrective action when what is being done does
not meet expectations

D. occurs after all the other managerial processes have been performed

19. The "brainstorming" technique for creative solutions of management problems MOST generally consists of   19. ...
    A. bringing staff together in an exchange of a quantity of free wheeling ideas
    B. isolating individual staff members to encourage thought
    C. developing improved office procedures
    D. preparation of written reports on complex problems

20. Computer systems hardware MOST often operates in relation   20. ...
to which one of the following steps in solving a data-processing problem?
    A. Determining the problem
    B. Defining and stating the problem
    C. Implementing the programmed solution
    D. Completing the documentation of every unexplored solution

21. There is a tendency in management to upgrade objectives.   21. ...
This trend is generally regarded as
    A. *desirable;* the urge to improve is demonstrated by adopting objectives that have been adjusted to provide improved service
    B. *undesirable;* the typical manager searches for problems which obstruct his objectives
    C. *desirable;* it is common for a manager to find that the details of an immediate operation have occupied so much of his time that he has lost sight of the basic overall objective
    D. *undesirable;* efforts are wasted when they are expended on a mass of uncertain objectives, since the primary need of most organizations is a single target or several major ones

22. Of the following, it is generally LEAST effective for an   22. ...
executive to delegate authority where working conditions involve
    A. rules establishing normal operating procedures
    B. consistent methods of operation
    C. rapidly changing work standards
    D. complex technology

23. If an executive was explaining the difficulty of making decisions under "risk" conditions, he would be MOST accurate   23. ...
if he said that such decisions would be difficult to make when the decision maker has
    A. limited information and experience and can expect many outcomes for each action
    B. much information and experience and can expect many outcomes for each action
    C. much information and experience and can expect few outcomes for each action
    D. limited information and experience and can expect few outcomes for each action

24. If an executive were asked to list some outstanding features of centralized organization, which one of the following would be INCORRECT? Centralized organization   24. ..
    A. lessens risks of errors by unskilled subordinates
    B. utilizes the skills of specialized experts at a central location

C. produces uniformity of policy and non-uniformity of action
D. enables closer control of operations than a decentralized set-up

25. It is possible for an organization's management to test whe- 25. ... ther or not the organization has a sound structure. Of the following, which one is NOT a test of soundness in an organization's structure? The
    A. ability to replace key personnel with minimum loss of effectiveness
    B. ability of information and decisions to flow more freely through the "grapevine" than through formal channels
    C. presence of definite objectives for each unit in the organizational system
    D. provision for orderly organizational growth with the ability to handle change as the need arises

TEST 2

1. Management experts generally believe that computer-based man- 1. ... agement information systems (MIS) have greater potential for improving the process of management than any other development in recent decades. The one of the following which MOST accurately describes the objectives of MIS is to
    A. provide information for decision-making on planning, initiating, and controlling the operations of the various units of the organization
    B. establish mechanization of routine functions such as clerical records, payroll, inventory and accounts receivable in order to promote economy and efficiency
    C. computerize decision-making on planning, initiative, organizing and controlling the operations of an organization
    D. provide accurate facts and figures on the various programs of the organization to be used for purposes of planning and research

2. The one of the following which is the BEST application of the 2. ... "management-by-exception" principle is that this principle
    A. stimulates communication and aids in management of crisis situations, thus reducing the frequency of decision-making
    B. saves time and reserves top-management decisions only for crisis situations, thus reducing the frequency of decision-making
    C. stimulates communication, saves time and reduces the frequency of decision-making
    D. is limited to crisis-management situations

3. It is *generally* recognized that each organization is depen- 3. ... dent upon the availability of qualified personnel. Of the following, the MOST important factor affecting the availability of qualified people to each organization is
    A. innovations in technology and science
    B. the general decline in the educational levels of our population
    C. the rise of sentiment against racial discrimination
    D. pressure by organized community groups

5

4. A *fundamental* responsibility of all managers is to decide what 4. ...
physical facilities and equipment are needed to help attain
basic goals. Good planning for the purchase and use of equipment is seldom easy to do and is *complicated* MOST by the fact
that
   A. organizations rarely have stable sources of supply
   B. nearly all managers tend to be better at personnel plan-
      ning than at equipment planning
   C. decisions concerning physical resources are made too of-
      ten on a "crash basis" rather than under carefully pre-
      pared policies
   D. legal rulings relative to depreciation fluctuate very
      frequently

5. In attempting to reconcile managerial objectives and an indi- 5. ...
vidual employee's goals, it is generally LEAST desirable for
management to
   A. recognize the capacity of the individual to contribute
      toward realization of managerial goals
   B. encourage self-development of the employee to exceed
      minimum job performance
   C. consider an individual employee's work separately from
      other employees
   D. demonstrate that an employee advances only to the extent
      that he contributes directly to the accomplishment of
      stated goals

6. As a management tool for discovering individual training needs, 6. ...
a job analysis would generally be of LEAST assistance in de-
termining
   A. the performance requirements of individual jobs
   B. actual employee performance on the job
   C. acceptable standards of performance
   D. training needs for individual jobs

7. One of the major concerns of organizational managers today is 7. ...
how the spread of automation will affect them and the status
of their positions. Realistically speaking, one can say that
the MOST likely effect of our newer forms of highly automated
technology on managers will be to
   A. make most top-level positions superfluous or obsolete
   B. reduce the importance of managerial work in general
   C. replace the work of managers with the work of technicians
   D. increase the importance of and demand for top managerial
      personnel

8. Which one of the following is LEAST likely to be an area or 8. ...
cause of trouble in the use of staff people (e.g., assistants
to the administrator)?
   A. Misunderstanding of the role the staff people are supposed
      to play, as a result of vagueness of definition of their
      duties and authority
   B. Tendency of staff personnel almost always to be older than
      line personnel at comparable salary levels with whom they
      must deal
   C. Selection of staff personnel who fail to have simultane-
      ously both competence in their specialties and skill in
      staff work
   D. The staff person fails to understand mixed staff and oper-
      ating duties

9. The one of the following which is the BEST measure of decen-   9. ...
tralization in an agency is the
   A. amount of checking required on decisions made at lower
     levels in the chain of command
   B. amount of checking required on decisions made at lower
     levels of the chain of command and the number of functions
     affected thereby
   C. number of functions affected by decisions made at higher
     levels
   D. number of functions affected by middle echelon decision-
     making

10. Which of the following is generally NOT a valid statement   10. ...
with respect to the supervisory process?
   A. General supervision is more effective than close super-
     vision.
   B. Employee-centered supervisors lead more effectively
     than do production-centered supervisors.
   C. Employee satisfaction is directly related to productivi-
     ty.
   D. Low-producing supervisors use techniques that are differ-
     ent from high-producing supervisors.

11. The one of the following which is the MOST essential element 11. ...
for proper evaluation of the performance of subordinate super-
visors is a
   A. careful definition of each supervisor's specific job re-
     sponsibilities and of his progress in meeting mutually
     agreed upon work goals
   B. system of rewards and penalties based on each supervi-
     sor's progress in meeting clearly defined performance
     standards
   C. definition of personality traits, such as industry, in-
     itiative, dependability and cooperativeness, required
     for effective job performance
   D. breakdown of each supervisor's job into separate com-
     ponents and a rating of his performance on each indi-
     vidual task

12. The one of the following which is the PRINCIPAL advantage of 12. ...
specialization for the operating efficiency of a public ser-
vice agency is that specialization
   A. reduces the amount of red tape in coordinating the acti-
     vities of mutually dependent departments
   B. simplifies the problem of developing adequate job controls
   C. provides employees with a clear understanding of the re-
     lationship of their activities to the overall objectives
     of the agency
   D. reduces destructive competition for power between depart-
     ments

13. Of the following, the group which *generally* benefits MOST   13. ...
from supervisory training programs in public service agencies
are those supervisors who have
   A. accumulated a long period of total service to the agency
   B. responsibility for a large number of subordinate personnel
   C. been in the supervisory ranks for a long period of time
   D. a high level of formalized academic training

14. A list of conditions which encourages good morale inside a 14. ...
    work group would NOT include a
    A. high rate of agreement among group members on values
       and objectives
    B. tight control system to minimize the risk of individual
       error
    C. good possibility that joint action will accomplish goals
    D. past history of successful group accomplishment

15. Of the following, the MOST important factor to be considered 15. ...
    in selecting a training strategy or program is the
    A. requirements of the job to be performed by the trainees
    B. educational level or prior training of the trainees
    C. size of the training group
    D. quality and competence of available training specialists

16. Of the following, the one which is considered to be LEAST 16. ...
    characteristic of the higher ranks of management is
    A. that higher levels of management benefit from modern
       technology
    B. that success is measured by the extent to which objec-
       tives are achieved
    C. the number of subordinates that directly report to an
       executive
    D. the deemphasis of individual and specialized performance

17. Assume that an executive is preparing a training syllabus 17. ...
    to be used in training members of his staff. Which of the
    following would NOT be a valid principle of the learning pro-
    cess for this manager to keep in mind in the preparation of
    the training syllabus?
    A. When a person has thoroughly learned a task, it takes
       a lot of effort to create a little more improvement
    B. In complicated learning situations, there is a period
       in which an additional period of practice produces an
       equal amount of improvement in learning
    C. The less a person knows about the task, the slower the
       initial progress
    D. The more the person knows about the task, the slower
       the initial progress

18. Of the following, which statement BEST illustrates when col- 18. ...
    lective bargaining agreements are working well?
    A. Executives strongly support subordinate managers.
    B. The management rights clause in the contract is clear
       and enforced.
    C. Contract provisions are competently interpreted.
    D. The provisions of the agrement are properly interpreted,
       communicated and observed.

19. An executive who wishes to encourage subordinates to commu- 19. ...
    nicate freely with him about a job-related problem should
    FIRST
    A. state his own position on the problem before listening
       to the subordinates' ideas
    B. invite subordinates to give their own opinions on the
       problem
    C. ask subordinates for their reactions to his own ideas
       about the problem
    D. guard the confidentiality of management information
       about the problem

20. The ability to deal constructively with intra-organization- 20. ...
    al conflict is an essential attribute of the successful mana-
    ger. The one of the following types of conflict whcch would
    be LEAST difficult to handle constructively is a situation
    in which there is
    A. agreement on objectives, but disagreement as to the pro-
       bable results of adopting the various alternatives
    B. agreement on objectives, disagreement on alternative
       courses of action, and relative certainty as to the out-
       come of one of the alternatives
    C. disagreement on objectives and on alternative courses of
       action, but relative certainty as to the outcome of the
       alternatives
    D. disagreement on objectives and on alternative courses of
       action, but uncertainty as to the outcome of the alterna-
       tives

21. Which of the following statements is LEAST accurate in de- 21. ...
    scribing formal job evaluation and wage and salary classifi-
    cation plans?
    A. Parties that disagree on wage matters can examine an es-
       tablished system rather than unsupported opinions.
    B. The use of such plans tends to overlook the effect of
       age and seniority of employees on job values in the plan
    C. Such plans can eliminate salary controversies in organi-
       zations designing and using them properly
    D. These plans are not particularly useful in checking on
       executive compensation

22. In carrying out disciplinary action, the MOST important pro-22. ...
    cedure for all managers to follow is to
    A. sell all levels of management on the need for discipline
       from the organization's viewpoint
    B. follow up on a disciplinary action and not assume that
       the action has been effective
    C. convince all executives that proper discipline is a
       legitimate tool for their use
    D. convince all executives that they need to display con-
       fidence in the organization's rules

Questions 23-25.
DIRECTIONS: Questions 23 through 25 are based on the following situation.
   Richard Ford, a top administrator, is responsible for output in his
organization. Because productivity had been lagging for two periods in
a row, Ford decided to establish a committee of his subordinate managers
to investigate the reasons for the poor performance and to make recommendations for improvements. After two meetings, the committee came to
the conclusions and made the recommendations that follow:
   Output forecasts had been handed down from the top without prior consultation with middle management and first level supervision. Lines of
authority and responsibility had been unclear. The planning and control
process should be decentralized.
   After receiving the committee's recommendations, Ford proceeded to
take the following actions:
   Ford decided he would retain final authority to establish quotas but
would delegate to the middle managers the responsibility for meeting
quotas.

After receiving Ford's decision, the middle managers proceeded to delegate to the first-line supervisors the authority to establish their own quotas. The middle managers eventually received and combined the first-line supervisors' quotas so that these conformed with Ford's.

23. Ford's decision to delegate responsibility for meeting quotas   23. ...
    to the middle managers is INCONSISTENT with sound management
    principles because of which one of the following?
    A. Ford shouldn't have involved himself in the first place.
    B. Middle managers do not have the necessary skills.
    C. Quotas should be established by the chief executive.
    D. Responsibility should not be delegated.
24. The principle of coextensiveness of responsibility and au-   24. ...
    thority bears on Ford's decision. In this case, it IMPLIES that
    A. authority should exceed responsibility
    B. authority should be delegated to match the degree of
       responsibility
    C. both authority and responsibility should be retained
       and not delegated
    D. responsibility should be delegated but authority should
       be retained
25. The middle managers' decision to delegate to the first-line   25. ...
    supervisors the authority to establish quotas was INCORRECTLY
    reasoned because
    A. delegation and control must go together
    B. first-line supervisors are in no position to establish
       quotas
    C. one cannot delegate authority that one does not possess
    D. the meeting of quotas should not be delegated

TEST 3

1. A danger which exists in any organization as complex as that   1. ...
   required for administration of a large public agency, is that
   each department comes to believe that it exists for its own
   sake.
   The one of the following which has been attempted in some or-
   ganizations as a cure for this condition is to
   A. build up the departmental esprit de corps
   B. expand the functions and jurisdictions of the various de-
      partments so that better integration is possible
   C. develop a body of specialists in the various subject mat-
      ter fields which cut across departmental lines
   D. delegate authority to the lowest possible echelon
   E. systematically transfer administrative personnel from one
      department to another
2. At best, the organization chart is ordinarily and necessarily   2. ...
   an idealized picture of the intent of top management, a reflec-
   tion of hopes and aims rather than a photograph of the operat-
   ing facts within the organization.
   The one of the following which is the basic reason for this is
   that the organization chart
   A. does not show the flow of work within the organization
   B. speaks in terms of positions rather than of live employees
   C. frequently contains unresolved internal ambiguities

10

D. is a record of past organization or of proposed future organization and never a photograph of the living organization

E. does not label the jurisdiction assigned to each component unit

3. The drag of inadequacy is always downward. The need in admin- 3. ...
istration is always for the reverse; for a department head to project his thinking to the city level, for the unit chief to try to see the problems of the department.
The inability of a city administration to recruit administrators who can satisfy this need usually results in departments characterized by
   A. disorganization   B. poor supervision
   C. circumscribed viewpoints   D. poor public relations
   E. a lack of programs

4. When, as a result of a shift in public sentiment, the elective 4. ...
officers of a city are changed, is it desirable for career administrators to shift ground without performing any illegal or dishonest act in order to conform to the policies of the new elective officers?
   A. *No;* the opinions and beliefs of the career officials are the result of long experience in administration and are more reliable than those of politicians.
   B. *Yes;* only in this way can citizens, political officials and career administrators alike have confidence in the performance of their respective functions.
   C. *No;* a top career official who is so spineless as to change his views or procedures as a result of public opinion is of little value to the public service.
   D. *Yes;* legal or illegal, it is necessary that a city employee carry out the orders of his superior officers
   E. *No;* shifting ground with every change in administration will preclude the use of a constant over-all policy

5. Participation in developing plans which will affect levels in 5. ...
the organization in addition to his own, will contribute to an individual's understanding of the entire system. When possible, this should be encouraged.
This policy, is, in general,
   A. *desirable;* the maintenance of any organization depends upon individual understanding
   B. *undesirable;* employees should participate only in thise activities which affect their own level, otherwise conflicts in authority may arise
   C. *desirable;* an employee's will to contribute to the maintenance of an organization depends to a great extent on the level which he occupies
   D. *undesirable;* employees can be trained more efficiently and economically in an organized training program than by participating in plan development
   E. *desirable;* it will enable the employee to make intelligent suggestions for adjustment of the plan in the future

6. Constant study should be made of the information contained in 6. ...
reports to isolate those elements of experience which are static, those which are variable and repetitive, and those which are variable and due to chance.

Knowledge of those elements of experience in his organization which are static or constant will enable the operating official to

    A. fix responsibility for their supervision at a lower level
    B. revise the procedure in order to make the elements variable
    C. arrange for follow-up and periodic adjustment
    D. bring related data together
    E. provide a frame of reference within which detailed standards for measurement can be installed

7. A chief staff officer, serving as one of the immediate advisors 7. ...
to the department head, has demonstrated a special capacity for achieving internal agreements and for sound judgment. As a result he has been used more and more as a source of counsel and assistance by the department head. Other staff officers and line officials as well have discovered that it is wise for them to check with this colleague in advance on all problematical matters handed up to the department head. Developments such as this are

    A. *undesirable;* they disrupt the normal lines for flow of work in an organization
    B. *desirable;* they allow an organization to make the most of its strength wherever such strength resides
    C. *undesirable;* they tend to undermine the authority of the department head and put it in the hands of a staff officer who does not have the responsibility
    D. *desirable;* they tend to resolve internal ambiguities in organization
    E. *undesirable;* they make for bad morale by causing "cut-throat" competition

8. A common difference among executives is that some are not con- 8. ...
tent unless they are out in front in everything that concerns their organization, while others prefer to run things by pulling strings, by putting others out in front and by stepping into the breach only when necessary.
Generally speaking, an advantage this latter method of operation has over the former is that it

    A. results in a higher level of morale over a sustained period of time
    B. gets results by exhortation and direct stimulus
    C. makes it unnecessary to calculate integrated moves
    D. makes the personality of the executive felt further down the line
    E. results in the executive getting the reputation for being a good fellow

9. Administrators frequently have to get facts by interviewing   9. ...
people. Although the interview is a legitimate fact gathering technique, it has definite limitations which should not be overlooked. The one of the following which is an important limitation is that

    A. people who are interviewed frequently answer questions with guesses rather than admit their ignorance
    B. it is a poor way to discover the general attitude and thinking of supervisors interviewed
    C. people sometimes hesitate to give information during an interview which they will submit in written form

    D. it is a poor way to discover how well employees under-
       stand departmental policies
    E. the material obtained from the interview can usually be
       obtained at lower cost from existing records

10. It is desirable and advantageous to leave a maximum measure   10. ...
of planning responsibility to operating agencies or units, rather than to remove the responsibility to a central planning
staff agency.
Adoption of the former policy (decentralized planning) would
lead to

    A. *less effective planning;* operating personnel do not have
       the time to make long-term plans
    B. *more effective planning;* operating units are usually bet-
       ter equipped technically than any staff agency and conse-
       quently are in a better position to set up valid plans
    C. *less effective planning;* a central planning agency has a
       more objective point of view than any operating agency
       can achieve
    D. *more effective planning;* plans are conceived in terms of
       the existing situation and their exeuction is carried out
       with the will to succeed
    E. *less effective planning;* there is little or no opportuni-
       ty to check deviation from plans in the proposed set-up

Questions 11-15.
DIRECTIONS: The following sections appeared in a report on the work
          production of two bureaus of a department. Base your answers
          to questions 11 through 15 on this information. Throughout
          the report, assume that each month has 4 weeks.

Each of the two bureaus maintains a chronological file. In Bureau A,
every 9 months on the average, this material fills a standard legal size
file cabinet sufficient for 12,000 work units. In Bureau B, the same type
of cabinet is filled in 18 months. Each bureau maintains three complete
years of information plus a current file. When the current file cabinet
is filled, the cabinet containing the oldest material is emptied, the contents disposed of and the cabinet used for current material. The simi-
larity of these operations makes it possible to consolidate these files
with little effort.

Study of the practice of using typists as filing clerks for periods
when there is no typing work showed: (1) Bureau A has for the past 6
months completed a total of 1500 filing work units a week using on the
average 100 man-hours of trained file clerk time and 20 man-hours of
typist time; (2) Bureau B has in the same period completed a total of
2000 filing work units a week using on the average 125 man-hours of
trained file clerk time and 60 hours of typist time. This includes all
work in chronological files. Assuming that all clerks work at the same
speed and that all typists work at the same speed, this indicates that
work other than filing should be found for typists or that they should
be given some training in the filing procedures used... It should be
noted that Bureau A has not been producing the 1,600 units of technical
(not filing) work per 30 day period required by Schedule K, but is at
present 200 units behind. The Bureau should be allowed 3 working days
to get on schedule.

11. What percentage (approximate) of the total number of filing   11. ...
    work units completed in both units consists of the work in-
    volved in the maintenance of the chronological files?
        A. 5%   B. 10%   C. 15%   D. 20%   E. 25%

12. If the two chronological files are consolidated, the number   12. ...
    of months which should be allowed for filling a cabinet is
        A. 2   B. 4   C. 6   D. 8   E. 14

13. The MAXIMUM number of file cabinets which can be released   13. ...
    for other uses as a result of the consolidation recommended is
        A. 0   B. 1   C. 2   D. 3
        E. not determinable on the basis of the data given

14. If all the filing work for both units is consolidated without 14. ...
    diminution in the amount to be done and all filing work is
    done by trained file clerks, the number of clerks required
    (35-hour work week) is
        A. 4   B. 5   C. 6   D. 7   E. 8

15. In order to comply with the recommendation with respect to   15. ...
    Schedule K, the present work production of Bureau A must be
    increased by
        A. 50%   B. 100%   C. 150%   D. 200%
        E. an amount which is not determinable

16. A certain training program during World War II resulted in   16. ...
    the training of thousands of supervisors in industry. The
    methods of this program were later successfully applied in
    various governmental agencies. The program was based upon the
    assumption that there is an irreducible minimum of three su-
    pervisory skills. The ONE of these skills among the following
    is
        A. to know how to perform the job at hand well
        B. to be able to deal personally with workers, especially
           face to face
        C. to be able to imbue workers with the will to perform
           the job well
        D. to know the kind of work that is done by one's unit and
           the policies and procedures of one's agency
        E. the "know-how" of administrative and supervisory processes

17. A comment made by an employee about a training course was, "We 17. ...
    never have any idea how we are getting along in that course."
    The fundamental error in training methods to which this criti-
    cism points is
        A. insufficient student participation
        B. failure to develop a feeling of need or active want for
           the material being presented
        C. the training sessions may be too long
        D. no attempt may have been made to connect the new material
           with what was already known
        E. no goals have been set for the students

18. Assume that you are attending a departmental conference on   18. ...
    efficiency ratings at which it is proposed that a man-to-man
    rating scale be introduced. You should point out that, of the
    following, the CHIEF weakness of the man-to-man rating scale
    is that
        A. it involves abstract numbers rather than concrete employ-
           ee characteristics
        B. judges are unable to select their own standards for com-
           parison

C. the standard for comparison shifts from man to man for each person rated

D. not every person rated is given the opportunity to serve as a standard for comparison

E. standards for comparison will vary from judge to judge

19. Assume that you are conferring with a supervisor who has as- 19. ...
signed to his subordinates efficiency ratings which you believe to be generally too low. The supervisor argues that his ratings are generally low because his subordinates are generally inferior. Of the following, the evidence MOST relevant to the point at issue can be secured by comparing efficiency ratings assigned by the supervisor

A. with ratings assigned by other supervisors in the same agency

B. this year with ratings assigned by him in previous years

C. to men recently transferred to his unit with ratings previously earned by these men

D. with the general city average of ratings assigned by all supervisors to all employees

E. with the relative order of merit of his employees as determined independently by promotion test marks

20. The one of the following which is NOT among the most common 20. ...
of the compensable factors used in wage evaluation studies is

A. initiative and ingenuity required

B. physical demand

C. responsibility for the safety of others

D. working conditions

E. presence of avoidable hazards

21. If independent functions are separated, there is an immediate 21. ...
gain in conserving special skills. If we are to make optimum use of the abilities of our employees, these skills must be conserved.

Assuming the correctness of this statement, it follows that

A. if we are not making optimum use of employee abilities, independent functions have not been separated

B. we are making optimum use of employee abilities if we conserve special skills

C. we are making optimum use of employee abilities if independent functions have been separated

D. we are not making optimum use of employee abilities if we do not conserve special skills

E. if special skills are being conserved, independent functions need not be separated

22. A reorganization of the bureau to provide for a stenograph- 22. ...
ic pool instead of individual unit stenographers will result in more stenographic help being available to each unit when it is required, and consequently will result in greater productivity for each unit. An analysis of the space requirements shows that setting up a stenographic pool will require a minimum of 400 square feet of good space. In order to obtain this space, it will be necessary to reduce the space available for technical personnel, resulting in lesser productivity for each unit.

On the basis of the above discussion, it can be stated that, in order to obtain greater productivity for each unit,

     A. a stenographic pool should be set up
     B. further analysis of the space requirement should be made
     C. it is not certain as to whether or not a stenographic pool should be set up
     D. the space available for each technician should be increased in order to compensate for the absence of a stenographic pool
     E. a stenographic pool should not be set up

23. The adoption of a single consolidated form will mean that most 23. . . of the form will not be used in any one operation. This would create waste and confusion.

    This conclusion is based upon the unstated hypothesis that
     A. if waste and confusion are to be avoided, a single consolidated form should be used
     B. if a single consolidated form is constructed, most of it can be used in each operation
     C. if waste and confusion are to be avoided, most of the form employed should be used
     D. most of a single consolidated form is not used
     E. a single consolidated form should not be used

———

KEY (CORRECT ANSWERS)

TEST 1				TEST 2				TEST 3			
1.	A	11.	B	1.	A	11.	A	1.	E	11.	C
2.	C	12.	D	2.	C	12.	B	2.	B	12.	C
3.	B	13.	D	3.	A	13.	D	3.	C	13.	B
4.	A	14.	C	4.	C	14.	B	4.	B	14.	D
5.	B	15.	C	5.	C	15.	A	5.	E	15.	E
6.	D	16.	A	6.	B	16.	C	6.	A	16.	B
7.	B	17.	B	7.	D	17.	D	7.	B	17.	E
8.	B	18.	D	8.	B	18.	D	8.	A	18.	E
9.	C	19.	A	9.	B	19.	B	9.	A	19.	C
10.	A	20.	C	10.	C	20.	B	10.	D	20.	E
		21.	A			21.	C			21.	D
		22.	C			22.	B			22.	C
		23.	A			23.	D			23.	C
		24.	C			24.	B				
		25.	B			25.	C				

EXAMINATION SECTION
TEST 1

DIRECTIONS: Each question or incomplete statement is followed by several suggested answers or completions. Select the one that BEST answers the question or completes the statement. *PRINT THE LETTER OF THE CORRECT ANSWER IN THE SPACE AT THE RIGHT.*

1. An executive assigns A, the head of a staff unit, to devise plans for reducing the delay in   1._____
submittal of reports by a local agency headed by C. The reports are under the supervision of C's subordinate line official B with whom A is to deal directly. In his investigation, A finds: (1) the reasons for the delay; and (2) poor practices which have either been overlooked or condoned by line official B.
Of the following courses of action A could take, the BEST one would be to

   A. develop recommendations with line official B with regard to reducing the delay and correcting the poor practices and then report fully to his own executive
   B. discuss the findings with C in an attempt to correct the situation before making any formal report on the poor practices
   C. report both findings to his executive, attaching the explanation offered by C
   D. report to his executive on the first finding and discuss the second in a friendly way with line official B
   E. report the first finding to his executive, ignoring the second until his opinion is requested

2. Drafts of a proposed policy, prepared by a staff committee, are circulated to ten members   2._____
of the field staff of the organization by route slips with a request for comments within two weeks. Two members of the field staff make extensive comments, four offer editorial suggestions and the remainder make minor favorable comments. Shortly after, it found that the statement needs considerable revision by the field staff.
Of the following possible reasons for the original failure of the field staff to identify difficulties, the MOST likely is that the

   A. field staff did not take sufficient time to review the material
   B. field staff had not been advised of the type of contribution expected
   C. low morale of the field staff prevented their showing interest
   D. policy statement was too advanced for the staff
   E. staff committee was not sufficiently representative

3. Operator participation in management improvement work is LEAST likely to   3._____

   A. assure the use of best available management technique
   B. overcome the stigma of the outside expert
   C. place responsibility for improvement in the person who knows the job best
   D. simplify installation
   E. take advantage of the desire of most operators to seek self-improvement

4. In general, the morale of workers in an agency is MOST frequently and MOST signifi-   4._____
cantly affected by the

A. agency policies of organizational structure and operational procedures
B. distance of the employee's job from his home community
C. fringe benefits
D. number of opportunities for advancement
E. relationship with supervisors

5. Of the following, the PRIMARY function of a work distribution chart is to   5.____

   A. analyze the soundness of existing divisions of labor
   B. eliminate unnecessary clerical detail
   C. establish better supervisory techniques
   D. simplify work methods
   E. weed out core functions

6. In analyzing a process chart, which one of the following should be asked FIRST?   6.____

   A. How   B. When   C. Where   D. Who   E. Why

7. Which one of the following is NOT an advantage of the interview method of collecting   7.____
data?
It

   A. enables interviewer to judge the person interviewed on such matters as general attitude, knowledge, etc.
   B. helps build up personal relations for later installation of changes
   C. is a flexible method that can be adjusted to changing circumstances
   D. permits the obtaining of *off the record* information
   E. produces more accurate information than other methods

8. Which one of the following may be defined as *a regularly recurring appraisal of the man-*   8.____
ner in which all elements of agency management are being carried out?

   A. Functional survey   B. Operations audit
   C. Organization survey   D. Over-all survey
   E. Reconnaissance survey

9. An analysis of the flow of work in a department should begin with the _____ work.   9.____

   A. major routine   B. minor routine
   C. supervisory   D. technical
   E. unusual

10. Which method would MOST likely be used to get first-hand information on complaints   10.____
from the public?

   A. Study of correspondence
   B. Study of work volume
   C. Tracing specific transactions through a series of steps
   D. Tracing use of forms
   E. Worker desk audit

11. People will generally produce the MOST if   11.____

   A. management exercises close supervision over the work
   B. there is strict discipline in the group

C.   they are happy in their work
D.   they feel involved in their work
E.   they follow *the one best way*

12. The normal analysis of which chart listed below is MOST closely related to organiza-   12.____
     tional analysis?
     _____ chart.

     A.   Layout   B.   Operation
     C.   Process   D.   Work count
     E.   Work distribution

13. The work count would be LEAST helpful in accomplishing which one of the following?   13.____

     A.   Demonstrating personnel needs
     B.   Improving the sequence of steps
     C.   Measuring the value of a step
     D.   Spotting bottlenecks
     E.   Stimulating interest in work

14. Which of the following seems LEAST useful as a guide in interviewing an employee in a   14.____
     procedure and methods survey?

     A.   Explaining who you are and the purpose of your visit
     B.   Having a general plan of what you intend to get from the interview
     C.   Listening carefully and not interrupting
     D.   Trying out his reactions to your ideas for improvements
     E.   Trying to analyze his reasons for saying what he says

15. Which one of the following is an advantage of the questionnaire method of gathering   15.____
     facts as compared with the interview method?

     A.   Different people may interpret the questions differently.
     B.   Less *off the record* information is given.
     C.   More time may be taken in order to give exact answers.
     D.   Personal relationships with the people involved are not established.
     E.   There is less need for follow-up.

16. Which one of the following is generally NOT an advantage of the personal observation   16.____
     method of gathering facts?
     It

     A.   enables staff to use *off the record* information if personally observed
     B.   helps in developing valid recommendations
     C.   helps the person making the observation acquire *know how* valuable for later
          installation and follow-up
     D.   is economical in time and money
     E.   may turn up other problems in need of solution

17. Which of the following would MOST often be the best way to minimize resistance to   17.____
     change?

     A.   Break the news about the change gently to the people affected.
     B.   Increase the salary of the people affected by the change.

C. Let the people concerned participate in arriving at the decision to change.
D. Notify all people concerned with the change, both orally and in writing.
E. Stress the advantages of the new system.

18. The functional organization chart 18.___

A. does not require periodic revision
B. includes a description of the duties of each organization segment
C. includes positions and titles for each organization segment
D. is the simplest type of organization chart
E. is used primarily by newly established agencies

19. The principle of span of control has frequently been said to be in conflict with the 19.___

A. principle of unity of command
B. principle that authority should be commensurate with responsibility
C. principle that like functions should be grouped into one unit
D. principle that the number of levels between the top of an organization and the bottom should be small
E. scalar principle

20. If an executive delegates to his subordinates authority to handle problems of a routine 20.___
nature for which standard solutions have been established, he may expect that

A. fewer complaints will be received
B. he has made it more difficult for his subordinates to solve these problems
C. he has opened the way for confusion in his organization
D. there will be a lack of consistency in the methods applied to the solution of these problems
E. these routine problems will be handled efficiently and he will have more time for other non-routine work

21. Which of the following would MOST likely be achieved by a change in the basic organiza- 21.___
tion structure from the *process* or *functional* type to the *purpose* or *product* type?

A. Easier recruitment of personnel in a tight labor market
B. Fixing responsibility at a lower level in the organization
C. Greater centralization
D. Greater economy
E. Greater professional development

22. Usually the MOST difficult problem in connection with a major reorganization is 22.___

A. adopting a pay plan to fit the new structure
B. bringing the organization manual up-to-date
C. determining the new organization structure
D. gaining acceptance of the new plan by the higher level employees
E. gaining acceptance of the new plan by the lower level employees

23. Which of the following statements MOST accurately describes the work of the chiefs of 23.___
MOST staff divisions in departments?
Chiefs

A. focus more on getting the job done than on how it is done
B. are mostly interested in short-range results
C. nearly always advise but rarely if ever command or control
D. usually command or control but rarely advise
E. provide service to the rest of the organization and/or assist the chief executive in planning and controlling operations

24. In determining the type of organization structure of an enterprise, the one factor that might be given relatively greater weight in a small organization than in a larger organization of the same nature is the

24.____

A. geographical location of the enterprise
B. individual capabilities of incumbents
C. method of financing to be employed
D. size of the area served
E. type of activity engaged in

25. Functional foremanship differs MOST markedly from generally accepted principles of administration in that it advocates

25.____

A. an unlimited span of control
B. less delegation of responsibility
C. more than one supervisor for an employee
D. nonfunctional organization
E. substitution of execution for planning

KEY (CORRECT ANSWERS)

1.	A		11.	D
2.	B		12.	E
3.	A		13.	B
4.	E		14.	D
5.	A		15.	C
6.	E		16.	D
7.	E		17.	C
8.	B		18.	B
9.	A		19.	D
10.	A		20.	E

21.	B
22.	D
23.	E
24.	B
25.	C

TEST 2

start at 16

DIRECTIONS: Each question or incomplete statement is followed by several suggested answers or completions. Select the one that BEST answers the question or completes the statement. *PRINT THE LETTER OF THE CORRECT ANSWER IN THE SPACE AT THE RIGHT*

1. Decentralization of the authority to make decisions is a necessary result of increased complexity in an organization, but for the sake of efficiency and coordination of operations, such decentralization must be planned carefully.
A good general rule is that

    A. any decision should be made at the lowest possible point in the organization where all the information and competence necessary for a sound decision are available
    B. any decision should be made at the highest possible point in the organization, thus guaranteeing the best decision
    C. any decision should be made at the lowest possible point in the organization, but always approved by management
    D. any decision should be made by management and referred to the proper subordinate for comment
    E. no decision should be made by any individual in the organization without approval by a superior

1.___

2. One drawback of converting a conventional consecutive filing system to a terminal digit filing system for a large installation is that

    A. conversion would be expensive in time and manpower
    B. conversion would prevent the proper use of recognized numeric classification systems, such as the Dewey decimal, in classifying files material
    C. responsibility for proper filing cannot be pinpointed in the terminal digit system
    D. the terminal digit system requires considerably more space than a normal filing system
    E. the terminal digit system requires long, specialized training on the part of files personnel

2.___

3. The basic filing system that would ordinarily be employed in a large administrative headquarters unit is the _____ file system.

    A. alphabetic   B. chronological
    C. mnemonic   D. retention
    E. subject classification

3.___

4. A records center is of benefit in a records management program primarily because

    A. all the records of the organization are kept in one place
    B. inactive records can be stored economically in less expensive storage areas
    C. it provides a place where useless records can be housed at little or no cost to the organization
    D. obsolete filing and storage equipment can be utilized out of view of the public
    E. records analysts can examine an organization's files without affecting the unit's operation or upsetting the supervisors

4.___

5. In examining a number of different forms to see whether any could be combined or elimi-   5.____
   nated, which of the following would one be MOST likely to use?

   A. Forms analysis sheet of recurring data
   B. Forms control log
   C. Forms design and approval request
   D. Forms design and guide sheet
   E. Numerical file

6. The MOST important reason for control of *bootleg* forms is that   6.____

   A. they are more expensive than authorized forms
   B. they are usually poorly designed
   C. they can lead to unnecessary procedures
   D. they cannot be reordered as easily as authorized forms
   E. violation of rules and regulations should not be allowed

7. With a box design of a form, the caption title or question to be answered should be   7.____
   located in the _____ of the box.

   A. center at the bottom   B. center at the top
   C. lower left corner   D. lower right corner
   E. upper left corner

8. A two-part snapout form would be MOST properly justified if   8.____

   A. it is a cleaner operation
   B. it is prepared ten times a week
   C. it saves time in preparation
   D. it is to be filled out by hand rather than by typewriter
   E. proper registration is critical

9. When deciding whether or not to approve a request for a new form, which reference is   9.____
   normally MOST pertinent?

   A. Alphabetical Forms File
   B. Functional Forms File
   C. Numerical Forms File
   D. Project completion report
   E. Records retention data

10. Which of the following statements BEST explains the significance of the famed Haw-   10.____
    thorne Plant experiments? They showed that

    A. a large span of control leads to more production than a small span of control
    B. morale has no relationship to production
    C. personnel counseling is of relatively little importance in a going organization
    D. the special attention received by a group in an experimental situation has a greater
       impact on production than changes in working conditions
    E. there is a direct relationship between the amount of illumination and production

11. Which of the following would most often NOT result from a highly efficient management   11.____
    control system?

A.   Facilitation of delegation
B.   Highlighting of problem areas
C.   Increase in willingness of people to experiment or to take calculated risks
D.   Provision of an objective test of new ideas or new methods and procedures
E.   Provision of information useful for revising objectives, programs, and operations

12.   The PERT system is a   12.___

A.   method for laying out office space on a modular basis utilizing prefabricated partitions
B.   method of motivating personnel to be continuously alert and to improve their appearance
C.   method of program planning and control using a network or flow plan
D.   plan for expanding reporting techniques
E.   simplified method of cost accounting

13.   The term *management control* is MOST frequently used to mean   13.___

A.   an objective and unemotional approach by management
B.   coordinating the efforts of all parts of the organization
C.   evaluation of results in relation to plan
D.   giving clear, precise orders to subordinates
E.   keeping unions from making managerial decisions

14.   Which one of the following factors has the MOST bearing on the frequency with which a   14.___
control report should be made?

A.   Degree of specialization of the work
B.   Degree of variability in activities
C.   Expense of the report
D.   Number of levels of supervision
E.   Number of personnel involved

15.   The value of statistical records is MAINLY dependent upon the   15.___

A.   method of presenting the material
B.   number of items used
C.   range of cases sampled
D.   reliability of the information used
E.   time devoted to compiling the material

16.   When a supervisor delegates an assignment, he should   16.___

A.   delegate his responsibility for the assignment
B.   make certain that the assignment is properly performed
C.   participate in the beginning and final stages of the assignment
D.   retain all authority needed to complete the assignment
E.   oversee all stages of the assignment

17. Assume that the department in which you are employed has never given official sanction to a mid-afternoon coffee break. Some bureaus have it and others do not. In the latter case, some individuals merely absent themselves for about 15 minutes at 3 P.M. while others remain on the job despite the fatigue which seems to be common among all employees in this department at that time.
The course of action which you should recommend, if possible, is to

    A. arrange a schedule of mid-afternoon coffee breaks for all employees
    B. forbid all employees to take a mid-afternoon coffee break
    C. permit each bureau to decide for itself whether or not it will have a coffee break
    D. require all employees who wish a coffee break to take a shorter lunch period
    E. arrange a poll to discover the consensus of the department

17.____

18. The one of the following which is LEAST important in the management of a suggestion program is

    A. giving awards which are of sufficient value to encourage competition
    B. securing full support from the department's officers and executives
    C. publicizing the program and the awards given
    D. holding special conferences to analyze and evaluate some of the suggestions needed
    E. providing suggestion boxes in numerous locations

18.____

19. The one of the following which is MOST likely to decrease morale is

    A. insistence on strict adherence to safety rules
    B. making each employee responsible for the tidiness of his work area
    C. overlooking evidence of hostility between groups of employees
    D. strong, aggressive leadership
    E. allocating work on the basis of personal knowledge of the abilities and interests of the members of the department

19.____

20. Assume that a certain office procedure has been standard practice for many years. When a new employee asks why this particular procedure is followed, the supervisor should FIRST

    A. explain that everyone does it that way
    B. explain the reason for the procedure
    C. inform him that it has always been done that way in that particular office
    D. tell him to try it for a while before asking questions
    E. tell him he has never thought about it that way

20.____

21. Several employees complain informally to their supervisor regarding some new procedures which have been instituted. The supervisor should IMMEDIATELY

    A. explain that management is responsible
    B. state frankly that he had nothing to do with it
    C. refer the matter to the methods analyst
    D. tell the employees to submit their complaint as a formal grievance
    E. investigate the complaint

21.____

22. A new employee asks his supervisor *how he is doing.* Actually, he is not doing well in   22.___
some phases of the job, but it is felt that he will learn in time.
The BEST response for the supervisor to make is:

    A. Some things you are doing well, and in others I am sure you will improve
    B. Wait until the end of your probationary period when we will discuss this matter
    C. You are not doing too well
    D. You are doing very well
    E. I'll be able to tell you when I go over your record

23. The PRINCIPAL aim of a supervisor is to   23.___

    A. act as liaison between employee and management
    B. get the work done
    C. keep up morale
    D. train his subordinates
    E. become chief of the department

24. When the work of two bureaus must be coordinated, direct contact between the subordi-   24.___
nates in each bureau who are working on the problem is

    A. *bad,* because it violates the chain of command
    B. *bad,* because they do not have authority to make decisions
    C. *good,* because it enables quicker results
    D. *good,* because it relieves their superiors of any responsibility
    E. *bad,* because they may work at cross purposes

25. Of the following, the organization defect which can be ascertained MOST readily merely   25.___
by analyzing an accurate and well-drawn organization chart is

    A. ineffectiveness of an activity
    B. improper span of control
    C. inappropriate assignment of functions
    D. poor supervision
    E. unlawful delegation of authority

KEY (CORRECT ANSWERS)

1.	A	11.	C
2.	A	12.	C
3.	E	13.	C
4.	B	14.	B
5.	A	15.	D
6.	C	16.	B
7.	E	17.	A
8.	E	18.	E
9.	B	19.	C
10.	D	20.	B

21.	E
22.	A
23.	B
24.	C
25.	B

———

EXAMINATION SECTION
TEST 1

DIRECTIONS: Each question or incomplete statement is followed by several suggested answers or completions. Select the one that BEST answers the question or completes the statement. *PRINT THE LETTER OF THE CORRECT ANSWER IN THE SPACE AT THE RIGHT.*

1. With a management staff of 15 capable analysts, which of the following organizational approaches would generally be BEST for overall results?
   Organization

   A. by specialists in fields, such as management, organization, systems analysis
   B. by clientele to be served, such as hospitals, police, education, social services
   C. where all 15 report directly to head of the management staff
   D. by specialized study groups with flexibility in assigning staff under a qualified project leader

1.____

2. In conducting a general management survey to identify problems and opportunities, which of the following would it be LEAST necessary to consider?

   A. Identifying program and planning deficiencies in each functional area
   B. Organization problems
   C. Sound management practices not being used
   D. The qualifications of the supervisory personnel

2.____

3. Which of the following statements MOST accurately defines *operations research?*

   A. A highly sophisticated system used in the analysis of management problems
   B. A specialized application of electronic data processing in the analysis of management problems
   C. Research on operating problems
   D. The application of sophisticated mathematical tools to the analysis of management problems

3.____

4. Theoretically, an ideal organization structure can be set up for each enterprise. In actual practice, the ideal organization structure is seldom, if ever, obtained. Of the following, the one that is of LEAST influence in determining the organization structure is the

   A. existence of agreements and favors among members of the organization
   B. funds available
   C. growing trend of management to discard established forms in favor of new forms
   D. opinions and beliefs of top executives

4.____

5. To which one of the following is it MOST important that the functional or technical staff specialist in a large organization devote major attention?

   A. Conducting audits of line operations
   B. Controlling of people in the line organization
   C. Developing improved approaches, plans, and procedures and assisting the line organization in their implementation
   D. Providing advice to his superior and to operating units

5.____

6. In the planning for reorganization of a department, which one of the following principles relating to the assignment of functions is NOT correct?

6.___

    A. Line and staff functions should be separated.
    B. Separate functions should be assigned to separate organizational units.
    C. There should be no disturbance of the previously assigned tasks of personnel.
    D. There should generally be no overlapping among organizational elements.

7. Results are BEST accomplished within an organization when the budgets and plans are developed by the

7.___

    A. budget office, independent of the operating units
    B. head of the operating unit based on analysis of prior year's operations after discussion with his superior
    C. head of the operating unit with general guidelines and data from higher authority and the budget office, and input from key personnel
    D. head of the organization unit based on an analysis of prior year's operations

8. The *management process* is a term used to describe the responsibilities common to

8.___

    A. all levels of management
    B. first line supervisors
    C. middle management jobs
    D. top management jobs

9. Of the following, committees are BEST used for

9.___

    A. advising the head of the organization
    B. improving functional work
    C. making executive decisions
    D. making specific planning decisions

10. Which of the following would NOT be a part of a management control system?

10.___

    A. An objective test of new ideas or methods in operation
    B. Determination of need for organization improvement
    C. Objective comparison of operating results
    D. Provision of information useful for revising objectives, programs, and operations

11. Of the following, the one which a line role generally does NOT include is

11.___

    A. controlling results and performance
    B. coordinating work and exchanging ideas with other line organizations
    C. implementation of approved plans developed by staff
    D. planning work and making operating decisions

12. In a normal curve, one standard deviation would include MOST NEARLY what percentage of the cases involved?

12.___

    A. 50%   B. 68%   C. 95%   D. 99%

13. The Office Layout Chart is a sketch of the physical arrangements of the office to which has been added the flow lines of the principal work performed there.
Which one of the following states the BEST advantage of superimposing the work flow onto the desk layout?

13.___

    A.   Lighting and acoustics can be improved.
    B.   Line and staff relationships can be determined.
    C.   Obvious misarrangements can be corrected.
    D.   The number of delays can be determined,

14. An advantage of the Multiple Process Chart over the Flow Process Chart is that the Multiple Process Chart shows the   14.____

    A.   individual worker's activity
    B.   number of delays
    C.   sequence of operations
    D.   simultaneous flow of work in several departments

15. Of the following, which is the MAJOR advantage of a microfilm record retention system?   15.____

    A.   Filing can follow the terminal digit system.
    B.   Retrieving documents from the files is faster.
    C.   Significant space is saved in storing records.
    D.   To read a microfilm record, a film reader is not necessary.

16. Which one of the following questions should the management analyst generally consider FIRST?   16.____

    A.   How is it being done? and Why should it be done that way?
    B.   What is being done? and Why is it necessary?
    C.   When should this job be done? and Why?
    D.   Who should do the job? and Why should he do it?

17. Assume that you are in the process of eliminating unnecessary forms.   17.____
The answer to which one of the following questions would be LEAST relevant?

    A.   Could the information be obtained elsewhere?
    B.   Is the form properly designed?
    C.   Is the form used as intended?
    D.   Is the purpose of the form essential to the operation?

18. Use of color in forms adds to their cost. Sometimes, however, the use of color will greatly simplify procedure and more than pay for itself in time saved and errors eliminated.
This is ESPECIALLY true when   18.____

    A.   a form passes through many reviewers
    B.   considerable sorting is required
    C.   the form is other than a standard size
    D.   the form will not be sent through the mail

19. Of the following techniques, the one GENERALLY employed and considered BEST in forms design is to divide writing lines into boxes with captions printed in small type _____ of the box,   19.____

    A.   centered in the lower part
    B.   centered in the upper part
    C.   in the upper lefthand corner
    D.   in the lower righthand corner

20. Many forms authorities advocate the construction of a functional forms file or index.   20.____
    If such a file is set up, the MOST effective way of classifying forms for such an index is
    classification by

    A. department
    B. form number
    C. name or type of form
    D. subject to which the form applies

21. An interrelated pattern of jobs which makes up the structure of a system is known as   21.____

    A. a chain of command
    B. cybernetics
    C. the formal organization
    D. the maintenance pattern

22. A transparent sheet of film containing multiple rows of microimages is characteristic of   22.____
    which one of the following types of microfilm?

    A. Aperture   B. Jacket
    C. Microfiche   D. Roll or reel

23. PRIMARY responsibility for training and development of employees generally rests with   23.____

    A. outside training agencies
    B. the individual who needs training
    C. the line supervisor
    D. the training specialist in the Personnel Office

24. Which of the following approaches usually provides the BEST communication in the   24.____
    objectives and values of a new program which is to be introduced?

    A. A general written description of the program by the program manager for review by
       those who share responsibility
    B. An effective verbal presentation by the program manager to those affected
    C. Development of the plan and operational approach in carrying out the program by
       the program manager assisted by his key subordinates
    D. Development of the plan by the program manager's supervisor

25. The term *total systems concept,* as used in electronic data processing, refers   25.____

    A. only to the computer and its associated electronic accessories
    B. only to the paper information output, or *software* aspect
    C. to a large computer-based information handling system, which supplies the infor-
       mation needs of an entire agency or corporation
    D. to all of the automated and manual information systems in a specific sub-division
       of an organization

26. Of the following, scientific management can BEST be considered as an attempt to estab-   26.____
    lish work procedures

    A. in fields of scientific endeavors
    B. which are beneficial only to bosses
    C. which require less control
    D. utilizing the concept of a man-machine system

27. The MAJOR failing of efficiency engineering was that it   27.____

    A.   overlooked the human factor
    B.   required experts to implement the techniques
    C.   was not based on true scientific principles
    D.   was too costly and time consuming

28. Which of the following organizations is MOST noted throughout the world for its training   28.____
in management?

    A.   American Management Association
    B.   American Political Science Association
    C.   Society for the Advancement of Management
    D.   Systems and Procedures Association

29. The GENERAL method of arriving at program objectives should be   29.____

    A.   a trial and error process
    B.   developed as the program progresses
    C.   included in the program plan
    D.   left to the discretion of the immediate supervisors

30. The review and appraisal of an organization to determine waste and deficiencies,   30.____
improved methods, better means of control, more efficient operations, and greater use of
human and physical facilities is known as a(n)

    A.   management audit
    B.   manpower survey
    C.   work simplification study
    D.   operations audit

31. When data are grouped into a frequency distribution, the *median* is BEST defined as the   31.____
_____ in the distribution.

    A.   50% point
    B.   largest single range
    C.   smallest single range
    D.   point of greatest concentration

32. The manual, visual, and mental elements into which an operation may be analyzed in   32.____
time and motion study are denoted by the term

    A.   measurement   B.   positioning
    C.   standards   D.   therbligs

33. Of the following, the symbol shown at the right, as used in a sys-   33.____
tems flow chart, denotes
    A.   decision
    B.   document
    C.   manual operation
    D.   process

34. Of the following agencies of city government, the one with the LARGEST expense budget for the current fiscal year is the   34

    A. environmental protection administration
    B. department of social services
    C. municipal service administration   previous
    D. police department

35. A feasibility study is the first phase in the process of conversion from manual to computerized data processing.   35.___
The phases, in sequence, are the feasibility study,

    A. system conversion, system installation, follow up
    B. system design, installation
    C. system design, follow up, installation
    D. system design, system conversion, installation

36.   36.___

NAME OF WORKER	1st Hour	2nd Hour	3rd Hour	4th Hour	5th Hour	6th Hour	7th Hour	8th Hour
J. Jones								
B. Brown								
R. Roe								

MONDAY

The type of chart illustrated above is generally known as a _____ Chart.

    A. Flow   B. Gantt
    C. Work Simplification   D. Motion-Time Study

37.   37.___

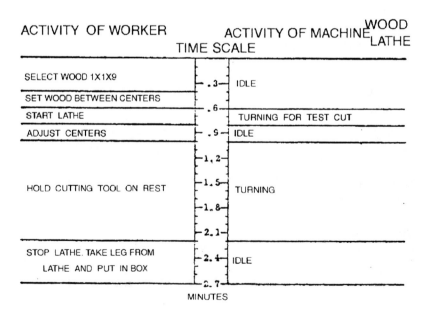

ACTIVITY OF WORKER	TIME SCALE	ACTIVITY OF MACHINE WOOD LATHE
SELECT WOOD 1X1X9	.3	IDLE
SET WOOD BETWEEN CENTERS	.6	
START LATHE		TURNING FOR TEST CUT
ADJUST CENTERS	.9	IDLE
HOLD CUTTING TOOL ON REST	1.2 / 1.5 / 1.8 / 2.1	TURNING
STOP LATHE. TAKE LEG FROM LATHE AND PUT IN BOX	2.4 / 2.7	IDLE

MINUTES

The type of chart illustrated on the previous page is generally known as a _____ Chart.

A. Flow
B. Gantt
C. Simo
D. Work Simplification

38.   38._____

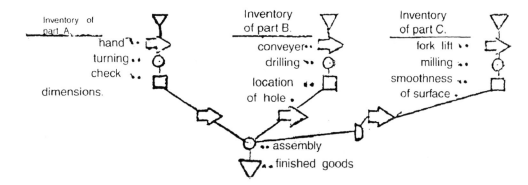

The type of chart illustrated above is generally known as a(n) _____ Chart.
A. Multiple Activity
B. Motion-Time
C. Work Place Layout
D. Operation Process

39._____

39.

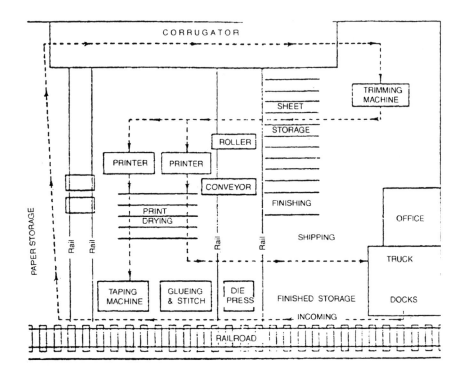

The one illustrated above is generally known as a

A. Gantt Chart
B. Multiple Activity Chart
C. Planned Flow Diagram
D. Work Place Diagram

40.

	PRESENT		PROPOSED		DIFFERENCE		
	NO.	Time	No.	Time	No.	Time	JOB
OPERATIONS							
TRANSPORTATIONS							
INSPECTIONS							
DELAYS							
STORAGES							
DISTANCE TRAVELLED		Ft.		Ft.		Ft.	

CHART BEGINS
CHART ENDS
CHARTED BY
DATE

DETAILS OF {PRESENT / PROPOSED} METHOD	OPERATION TRANSPORT INSPECTION DELAY STORAGE	DISTANCE BY FEET	TIME BY MINUTES	DETAILS OF {PRESENT / PROPOSED} METHOD	OPERATION TRANSPORT INSPECTION DELAY STORAGE	DISTANCE BY FEET	TIME BY MINUTES
1.	O ⇨ ☐ D ▽			1.	O ⇨ ☐ D ▽		
2.	O ⇨ ☐ D ▽			2.	O ⇨ ☐ D ▽		
3.	O ⇨ ☐ D ▽			3.	O ⇨ ☐ D ▽		
4.	O ⇨ ☐ D ▽			4.	O ⇨ ☐ D ▽		
5.	O ⇨ ☐ D ▽			5.	O ⇨ ☐ D ▽		
6.	O ⇨ ☐ D ▽			6.	O ⇨ ☐ D ▽		
7.	O ⇨ ☐ D ▽			7.	O ⇨ ☐ D ▽		
8.	O ⇨ ☐ D ▽			8.	O ⇨ ☐ D ▽		

The type of chart illustrated above is generally known as a(n) _____ Chart.

A. Analysis
C. Man or Material

B. Flow Process
D. Multiple Activity

———

KEY (CORRECT ANSWERS)

1.	D	11.	B	21.	C	31.	A
2.	D	12.	B	22.	C	32.	D
3.	D	13.	C	23.	C	33.	A
4.	C	14.	D	24.	C	34.	B
5.	C	15.	C	25.	C	35.	D
6.	C	16.	B	26.	D	36.	B
7.	C	17.	B	27.	A	37.	C
8.	A	18.	B	28.	A	38.	D
9.	A	19.	C	29.	C	39.	C
10.	B	20.	D	30.	A	40.	B

TEST 2

DIRECTIONS: Each question or incomplete statement is followed by several suggested answers or completions. Select the one that BEST answers the question or completes the statement. *PRINT THE LETTER OF THE CORRECT ANSWER IN THE SPACE AT THE RIGHT.*

1. The one of the following which is MOST important in getting a systems survey off to a good start is

    A. a kick-off meeting with key personnel covering the purpose of the study and introduction of the survey staff
    B. a prior knowledge of the organization manual, charts, and statements of responsibility
    C. knowledge of personality problems in the agency needing special attention
    D. written announcement from the agency head

1.____

2. Which of the following is the LEAST important factor in planning an administrative survey?

    A. Developing a work plan and time schedule
    B. Knowledge of sound organization concepts and principles
    C. Survey techniques and methods to be used for analysis in compiling data needed
    D. The purpose, scope, and level of the survey

2.____

3. Assume that a supervisor, when reviewing a decision reached by one of his subordinates, finds the decision incorrect.
Under these circumstances, it would be MOST desirable for the supervisor to

    A. correct the decision and inform the subordinate of this at a staff meeting
    B. correct the decision and suggest a more detailed analysis in the future
    C. help the employee find the reason for the correct decision
    D. refrain from assigning this type of problem to the employee

3.____

4. After an analyst has identified a problem area, which one of the following is the MOST important step in getting management to recognize that a problem does exist?

    A. A brief statement describing the problem
    B. Implications if problem is not corrected
    C. Relationship to other problems
    D. Supporting factual evidence and data indicating that the problem does exist

4.____

5. The statement, *work expands to fit the time available for its completion*, refers MOST directly to

    A. job enlargement principles
    B. Parkinson's Law
    C. The Open System Theory
    D. The Peter Principle

5.____

6. A comprehensive and constructive examination of a company, institution, or branch of government, or of any of its components such as an agency, division, or department, and its plans and objectives, methods of control, its means of operations, and its use of human and physical facilities is COMMONLY known as a(n) _____ audit.

    A. systems
    B. extensive financial
    C. operational or management
    D. organizational

7. Assume you are assigned to analyze the details of the procedures a clerk follows in order to complete filling out an invoice or a requisition. Your purpose is to simplify and shorten the procedure he has been trained to use.
The MOST appropriate chart for this purpose would be the

    A. block flow diagram   B. flow process chart
    C. forms flow chart   D. work distribution chart

8. In identifying problems and opportunities for improvement, which one of the following is MOST closely related to organization planning?

    A. Effective operating procedures issued from headquarters
    B. Effective records management
    C. Need for improved management concepts and practices
    D. Review of the salary and wage administration program

9. MOST of the working time of the functional or technical staff specialist in a large organization should be focused on

    A. conducting audits of line operations
    B. developing improved approaches, plans, and procedures and assisting the line organization in their implementation
    C. providing advice to his superior and to operating units
    D. the number of people in the line organization

10. The LEAST effective way for a survey group to plan is to

    A. clarify objectives and identify problems
    B. conduct planning and review sessions annually when budgets are prepared
    C. periodically conduct review sessions for purposes of coordination
    D. undertake specific action programs

11. Which one of the following is the MOST important element of a good manpower plan?

    A. Establishing inventories of capable personnel
    B. Forecasting the number of people needed in the future
    C. Having the right people for all jobs when needed
    D. Identifying training needs

12. Completed staff work is MOST effective in accomplishing which one of the following?

    A. Determination of the problems of the line organization
    B. Determination of the staffing needs of an organization
    C. Preparation of effective proposals and approaches to improve line results
    D. Review of budgets proposed by line organization

13. What generally is the PRINCIPAL objection to the use of form letters? 13.____
The

    A. difficulty of developing a form letter to serve the purpose
    B. excessive time involved in selecting the proper form letter
    C. errors in selecting form letters
    D. impersonality of form letters

14. What is the BEST approach for introducing change? 14.____
A

    A. combination of written and also verbal communication to all personnel affected by
       the change
    B. general bulletin to all personnel
    C. meeting pointing out all the values of the new approach
    D. written directive to key personnel

15. The FIRST step in designing an effective management survey is 15.____

    A. examining backlogs
    B. flow charting
    C. motion analysis and time study
    D. project planning

16. In statistical sampling, the error which will NOT be exceeded by 50 percent of the cases 16.____
is known as the

    A. difference between two means
    B. probable error
    C. standard deviation
    D. standard error of the mean

17. In a normal or bell-shaped curve, the area encompassed by two standard deviations 17.____
from the mean is

    A. 68%   B. 95%   C. 97%   D. 99%

18. The statistical average referring to that point on the scale at which the concentration is 18.____
greatest or that value which occurs the greatest number of times and which might be
taken as typical of the entire distribution is called the

    A. mean   B. median   C. mode   D. quartile

19. In process charting, the symbol which is used when con-ditions (except those which 19.____
intentionally change the physical or chemical characteristics of the object) do not permit
or require immediate performance is

    A.   B.   C.   D.

20. Assume that you are making a study of a central headquarters office which processes   20.____
    claims received from a number of district offices. You notice the following problems:
    Some employees are usually busy, while others doing the same kind of work in the same
    grade have little to do, high level professional people frequently spend considerable time
    searching for files in the file room. Which of the following charts would be MOST useful
    to record and analyze the data needed to help solve these problems?
    _____ Chart.

    A. Forms Distribution   B. Process
    C. Space Layout   D. Work Distribution

21. Which of the following types of work would NOT be readily measured by conventional   21.____
    time study techniques?
    Work

    A. of sufficient volume, uniform in nature, that will justify the cost of continuing and
        maintaining controls
    B. that is countable in precise quantitative terms
    C. that is essentially creative and considerably varied in content
    D. that is repetitive, uniform, and homogeneous in content over a period of time

22. Which of the following should be the FIRST consideration in a work simplification study?   22.____
    Can the

    A. sequence be changed for improvement?
    B. task be combined with another?
    C. task be eliminated?
    D. task be simplified?

23. In evaluating the sequence of operations involved in the clerical processing, which of the   23.____
    items listed below would be an indicator that methods improvements are needed?

    A. Some operations duplicate previous operations.
    B. The supervisor believes many of the company's policies are wrong.
    C. There is a high turnover of mail clerks.
    D. Work is logged into and out of the department.

24. Of the following, the one that is MOST likely to make a methods change unacceptable is   24.____
    when the

    A. change does not threaten the workers' security
    B. change follows a series of previously unsuccessful similar changes
    C. change has been well thought out and properly introduced
    D. people affected by the change have participated in the development of the
        changes

25. Which of the following questions has the LEAST significant bearing on the analysis of the   25.____
    paperwork flow?

    A. How is the work brought into the department and how is it taken away?
    B. How many work stations are involved in processing the work within the depart-
        ment?
    C. Is the work received and removed in the proper quantity?
    D. Where is the supervisor's desk located in relationship to those he supervises?

26. Which of the following does NOT have significant bearing on the arrangement, sequence, and zoning of information into box captions?
The

    A. layout of the source documents from which the infor-mation is taken
    B. logical flow of data
    C. needs of forms to be prepared from this form
    D. type of print to be employed

26.____

27. In determining the spacing requirements of a form and the size of the boxes to be used, PRIMARY consideration should be given to the

    A. distribution of the form
    B. method of entry, i.e., handwritten or machine and type of machine
    C. number of copies
    D. number of items to be entered

27.____

28. Of the following, the BEST technique to follow when providing instructions for the com-pletion and routing of a form is to _____ the form.

    A. imprint the instructions on the face of
    B. imprint the instructions on the back of
    C. provide a written procedure to accompany
    D. provide verbal instructions when issuing

28.____

29. A forms layout style where a separate space in the shape of a box is provided for each item of information requested and the caption or question for each item is shown in the upper lefthand corner of each box is known as the _____ style.

    A. box   B. checkbox
    C. checklist   D. checkbox and checklist

29.____

30. It is the office manager's responsibility to promote office safety and eliminate hazards. A number of policies and procedures are widely advocated and followed by management and safety experts.
Of the following, the policy or procedure that is LEAST valid is:

    A. Each department supervisor should be required to complete a report at the time of each accident so that the person in charge of safety administration will be able to analyze the pattern of common causes and improve safety conditions
    B. Electrical cords and connectors for machines and equipment should be routinely checked so as to eliminate fire and shock hazards
    C. Employees should be informed of the type of acci-dents which may occur
    D. Smoking at desks should be prohibited so as to avoid the possibility of fire hazards; and a lounge provided for this purpose

30.____

31. An effective discussion leader is one who

    A. announces the problem and his preconceived solution at the start of the discussion
    B. guides and directs the discussion according to pre-arranged outline
    C. interrupts or corrects confused participants to save time
    D. permits anyone to say anything at anytime

31.____

32. Under what circumstances would it be MOST advisable to have two or more clerks in a department share the same adding machine?
When

    A. capital appropriations are tight
    B. the clerks sharing the adding machine are located at adjacent desks
    C. the clerks sharing the adding machine get along with one another
    D. the need for the equipment is so little that there is negligible time lost in sharing the adding machine

32.____

33. Of the following, the statement that is MOST descriptive of, and fundamental to, proper office landscaping is:

    A. All clerical desks should be arranged singly and in rows
    B. The layout should be built around the flow of infor-mation and work in the office
    C. The layout should be built around the recognized organizational hierarchy of the office unit
    D. There should be many planters arranged to give the office an open look

33.____

34. The MOST significant factor to be considered in deciding on an electric typewriter is the

    A. ability of some electric typewriters to change type face
    B. prestige typists associate with an electric type-writer
    C. standardization of type face
    D. volume of work to be performed by the typist

34.____

35. The human relations movement in management theory is BASICALLY concerned with

    A. counteracting employee unrest
    B. eliminating the *time and motion* man
    C. interrelationships among individuals in organizations
    D. the psychology of the worker

35.____

36. PERT, as commonly used, stood for

    A. Periodic Estimate of Resource Trends
    B. Potential Energy Research Technology
    C. Professional Engineer Review Tests
    D. Program Evaluation and Review Technique

36.____

37. The BEST type of chart to use in showing the absolute movement or change of a contin-uous series of data over a period of time, such as changes in prices, employment or expenses, is usually a _____ chart.

    A. bar   B. line
    C. multiple bar   D. pie

37.____

38. A computer language that was ESPECIALLY designed for third generation computers to enable their capabilities to be effectively utilized is

    A. BASIC   B. COBOL   C. FORTRAN   D. PL/1

38.____

39. An analog computer computes by making measurements on

    A. a storage drum
    B. magnetic tape
    C. punched cards
    D. some parallel physical system

39._____

40. The ONLY basic arithmetic operations performed by digital computers are

    A. addition and subtraction
    B. addition, subtraction, multiplication, and division
    C. exponential equations
    D. multiplication and division

40._____

——————

KEY (CORRECT ANSWERS)

1.	A	11.	C	21.	C	31.	B
2.	B	12.	C	22.	C	32.	D
3.	C	13.	D	23.	A	33.	B
4.	D	14.	A	24.	B	34.	D
5.	B	15.	D	25.	D	35.	C
6.	C	16.	B	26.	D	36.	D
7.	B	17.	B	27.	B	37.	B
8.	C	18.	C	28.	A	38.	D
9.	B	19.	C	29.	A	39.	D
10.	B	20.	D	30.	D	40.	A

——————

COMMUNICATION
EXAMINATION SECTION

DIRECTIONS FOR THIS SECTION:
    Each question or incomplete statement is followed by several sug-
gested answers or completions. Select the one that BEST answers the
question or completes the statement. *PRINT THE LETTER OF THE CORRECT
ANSWER IN THE SPACE AT THE RIGHT.*

TEST 1

1. In some agencies the counsel to the agency head is given   1. ...
   the right to bypass the chain of command and issue orders
   directly to the staff concerning matters that involve certain specific processes and practices.
   This situation *most nearly* illustrates the PRINCIPLE of
       A. the acceptance theory of authority
       B. multiple - linear authority
       C. splintered authority   D. functional authority
2. It is commonly understood that communication is an impor-   2. ...
   tant part of the administrative process.
   Which of the following is NOT a valid principle of the
   communication process in administration?
       A. The channels of communication should be spontaneous
       B. The lines of communication should be as direct and
          as short as possible
       C. Communications should be authenticated
       D. The persons serving in communications centers should
          be competent
3. Of the following, the *one* factor which is generally con-   3. ...
   sidered LEAST essential to successful committee operations
   is
       A. stating a clear definition of the authority and scope
          of the committee
       B. selecting the committee chairman carefully
       C. limiting the size of the committee to four persons
       D. limiting the subject matter to that which can be
          handled in group discussion
4. Of the following, the FAILURE by line managers to accept   4. ...
   and appreciate the benefits and limitations of a new program or system *very frequently* can be traced to the
       A. budgetary problems involved
       B. resultant need to reduce staff
       C. lack of controls it engenders
       D. failure of top management to support its implementation
5. If a manager were thinking about using a committee of sub-   5. ...
   ordinates to solve an operating problem, which of the following would generally NOT be an *advantage* of such use of
   the committee approach?
       A. Improved coordination   B. Low cost
       C. Increased motivation   D. Integrated judgment
6. Every supervisor has many occasions to lead a conference   6. ...
   or participate in a conference of some sort.
   Of the following statements that pertain to conferences
   and conference leadership, which is generally considered
   to be MOST valid?
       A. Since World War II, the trend has been toward fewer
          shared decisions and more conferences.

1

    B. The most important part of a conference leader's job
       is to direct discussion.
    C. In providing opportunities for group interaction,
       management should avoid consideration of its past
       management philosophy.
    D. A good administrator cannot lead a good conference
       if he is a poor public speaker.

7. Of the following, it is usually LEAST desirable for a   7. ...
   conference leader to
    A. call the name of a person after asking a question
    B. summarize proceedings periodically
    C. make a practice of repeating questions
    D. ask a question without indicating who is to reply

8. Assume that, in a certain organization, a situation has   8. ...
   developed in which there is little difference in status
   or authority between individuals.
   Which of the following would be the *most likely* result
   with regard to COMMUNICATION in this organization?
    A. Both the accuracy and flow of communication will be
       improved.
    B. Both the accuracy and flow of communication will sub-
       stantially decrease.
    C. Employees will seek more formal lines of communication.
    D. Neither the flow nor the accuracy of communication
       will be improved over the former hierarchical structure.

9. The main function of many agency administrative officers 9. ...
   is "information management." Information that is received
   by an administrative officer may be classified as active
   or passive, depending upon whether or not it requires the
   recipient to take some action.
   Of the following, the item received which is *clearly* the
   MOST active information is
    A. an appointment of a new staff member
    B. a payment voucher for a new desk
    C. a press release concerning a past event
    D. the minutes of a staff meeting

10. Of the following, the one LEAST considered to be a com- 10. ...
   munication barrier is
    A. group feedback   B. charged words
    C. selective perception   D. symbolic meanings

11. Management studies support the hypothesis that, in spite 11. ...
   of the tendency of employees to censor the information
   communicated to their supervisor, subordinates are *more
   likely* to communicate problem-oriented information UPWARD
   when they have a
    A. long period of service in the organization
    B. high degree of trust in the supervisor
    C. high educational level
    D. low status on the organizational ladder

12. Electronic data processing equipment can produce more in- 12. ...
   formation faster than can be generated by any other means.
   In view of this, the *most important* PROBLEM faced by management at present is to
    A. keep computers fully occupied
    B. find enough computer personnel
    C. assimilate and properly evaluate the information

D. obtain funds to establish appropriate information systems

13. A well-designed management information system *essentially*   13. ...
    provides each executive and manager the INFORMATION he
    needs for
    A. determining computer time requirements
    B. planning and measuring results
    C. drawing a new organization chart
    D. developing a new office layout

14. It is generally agreed that management policies should be   14. ...
    periodically reappraised and restated in accordance with
    current conditions.
    Of the following, the approach which would be MOST effec-
    tive in determining whether a policy should be revised is
    to
    A. conduct interviews with staff members at all levels
       in order to ascertain the relationship between the
       policy and actual practice
    B. make proposed revisions in the policy and apply it
       to current problems
    C. make up hypothetical situations using both the old
       policy and a revised version in order to make compar-
       isons
    D. call a meeting of top level staff in order to discuss
       ways of revising the policy

15. Your superior has asked you to notify division employees   15. ...
    of an important change in one of the operating procedures
    described in the division manual. Every employee presently
    has a copy of this manual.
    Which of the following is normally the *most practical* way
    to get the employees to UNDERSTAND such a change?
    A. Notify each employee individually of the change and
       answer any questions he might have
    B. Send a written notice to key personnel, directing
       them to inform the people under them
    C. Call a general meeting, distribute a corrected page
       for the manual, and discuss the change
    D. Send a memo to employees describing the change in
       general terms and asking them to make the necessary
       corrections in their copies of the manual

16. Assume that the work in your department involves the use   16. ...
    of many technical terms.
    In such a situation, when you are answering inquiries
    from the general public, it would *usually* be BEST to
    A. use simple language and avoid the technical terms
    B. employ the technical terms whenever possible
    C. bandy technical terms freely, but explain each term
       in parentheses
    D. apologize if you are forced to use a technical term

17. Suppose that you receive a telephone call from someone   17. ...
    identifying himself as an employee in another city depart-
    ment who asks to be given information which your own de-
    partment regards as confidential.
    Which of the following is the BEST way of handling such a
    request?

3

A. Give the information requested, since your caller
   has official standing
B. Grant the request, provided the caller gives you a
   signed receipt
C. Refuse the request, because you have no way of knowing whether the caller is really who he claims to be
D. Explain that the information is confidential and inform the caller of the channels he must go through to
   have the information released to him

18. Studies show that office employees place high importance   18. ...
    on the social and human aspects of the organization. What
    office employees like best about their jobs is the kind of
    people with whom they work. So strive hard to group people
    who are most likely to get along well together.
    Based on this information, it is *most reasonable* to assume
    that office workers are MOST pleased to work in a group
    which
    A. is congenial   B. has high productivity
    C. allows individual creativity
    D. is unlike other groups

19. A certain supervisor does not compliment members of his   19. ...
    staff when they come up with good ideas. He feels that
    coming up with good ideas is part of the job and does not
    merit special attention.
    This supervisor's practice is
    A. *poor*, because recognition for good ideas is a good
       motivator
    B. *poor*, because the staff will suspect that the super-
       visor has no good ideas of his own
    C. *good*, because it is reasonable to assume that employ-
       ees will tell their supervisor of ways to improve
       office practice
    D. *good*, because the other members of the staff are not
       made to seem inferior by comparison

20. Some employees of a department have sent an anonymous   20. ...
    letter containing many complaints to the department head.
    Of the following, what is this *most likely* to show about
    the department?
    A. It is probably a good place to work.
    B. Communications are probably poor.
    C. The complaints are probably unjustified.
    D. These employees are probably untrustworthy.

21. Which of the following actions would usually be MOST AP-   21. ...
    PROPRIATE for a supervisor to take *after* receiving an
    instruction sheet from his superior explaining a new
    procedure which is to be followed?
    A. Put the instruction sheet aside temporarily until he
       determines what is wrong with the old procedure
    B. Call his superior and ask whether the procedure is
       one he must implement immediately
    C. Write a memorandum to the superior asking for more
       details
    D. Try the new procedure and advise the superior of any
       problems or possible improvements

22. Of the following, which one is considered the PRIMARY ad-   22. ...
    vantage of using a committee to resolve a problem in an
    organization?

4

    A. No one person will be held accountable for the decision
       since a group of people was involved
    B. People with different backgrounds give attention to
       the problem
    C. The decision will take considerable time so there is
       unlikely to be a decision that will later be regretted
    D. One person cannot dominate the decision-making process

23. Employees in a certain office come to their supervisor   23. ...
    with all their complaints about the office and the work.
    Almost every employee has had at least one minor complaint
    at some time.
    The situation with respect to complaints in this office
    may BEST be described as *probably*
    A. *good;* employees who complain care about their jobs and
       work hard
    B. *good;* grievances brought out into the open can be cor-
       rected
    C. *bad;* only serious complaints should be discussed
    D. *bad;* it indicates the staff does not have confidence
       in the administration

24. The administrator who allows his staff to suggest ways to   24. ...
    do their work will *usually* find that
    A. this practice contributes to high productivity
    B. the administrator's ideas produce greater output
    C. clerical employees suggest inefficient work methods
    D. subordinate employees resent performing a management
       function

25. The MAIN purpose for a supervisor's questioning the em-   25. ...
    ployees at a conference he is holding is to
    A. stress those areas of information covered but not
       understood by the participants
    B. encourage participants to think through the problem
       under discussion
    C. catch those subordinates who are not paying attention
    D. permit the more knowledgeable participants to display
       their grasp of the problems being discussed

TEST 2

1. For a superior to use *consultative supervision* with his   1. ...
   subordinates effectively, it is ESSENTIAL that he
    A. accept the fact that his formal authority will be
       weakened by the procedure
    B. admit that he does not know more than all his men
       together and that his ideas are not always best
    C. utilize a committee system so that the procedure is
       orderly
    D. make sure that all subordinates are consulted so
       that no one feels left out

2. The "grapevine" is an informal means of communication in   2. ...
   an organization.
   The attitude of a supervisor with respect to the grapevine should be to
    A. ignore it since it deals mainly with rumors and
       sensational information

B. regard it as a serious danger which should be eliminated

C. accept it as a real line of communication which should
be listened to

D. utilize it for most purposes instead of the official
line of communication

3. The supervisor of an office that must deal with the public   3. ...
should realize that planning in this type of work situation

A. is *useless* because he does not know how many people
will request service or what service they will request

B. *must be done at a higher level* but that he should be
ready to implement the results of such planning

C. is *useful* primarily for those activities that are not
concerned with public contact

D. is *useful* for all the activities of the office, including those that relate to public contact

4. Assume that it is your job to receive incoming telephone   4. ...
calls. Those calls which you cannot handle yourself have
to be transferred to the appropriate office.
If you receive an outside call for an extension line which
is busy, the one of the following which you should do FIRST
is to

A. interrupt the person speaking on the extension and
tell him a call is waiting

B. tell the caller the line is busy and let him know
every thirty seconds whether or not it is free

C. leave the caller on "hold" until the extension is free

D. tell the caller the line is busy and ask him if he
wishes to wait

5. Your superior has subscribed to several publications di-   5. ...
rectly related to your division's work, and he has asked
you to see to it that the publications are circulated among
the supervisory personnel in the division. There are eight
supervisors involved.
The BEST method of insuring that all eight see these publications is to

A. place the publication in the division's general reference library as soon as it arrives

B. inform each supervisor whenever a publication arrives
and remind all of them that they are responsible for
reading it

C. prepare a standard slip that can be stapled· to each
publication, listing the eight supervisors and saying,
"Please read, initial your name, and pass along"

D. send a memo to the eight supervisors saying that they
may wish to purchase individual subscriptions in their
own names if they are interested in seeing each issue

6. Your superior has telephoned a number of key officials in   6. ...
your agency to ask whether they can meet at a certain time
next month. He has found that they can all make it, and
he has asked you to confirm the meeting.
Which of the following is the BEST way to confirm such a
meeting?

A. Note the meeting on your superior's calendar

B. Post a notice of the meeting on the agency bulletin
board

C. Call the officials on the day of the meeting to remind
them of the meeting

D. Write a memo to each official involved, repeating the time and place of the meeting

7. Assume that a new city regulation requires that certain kinds of private organizations file information forms with your department. You have been asked to write the short explanatory message that will be printed on the front cover of the pamphlet containing the forms and instructions. Which of the following would be the MOST appropriate way of beginning this message?

    7. ...

    A. Get the readers' attention by emphasizing immediately that there are legal penalties for organizations that fail to file before a certain date
    B. Briefly state the nature of the enclosed forms and the types of organizations that must file
    C. Say that your department is very sorry to have to put organizations to such an inconvenience
    D. Quote the entire regulation adopted by the city, even if it is quite long and is expressed in complicated legal language

8. Suppose that you have been told to make up the vacation schedule for the 18 employees in a particular unit. In order for the unit to operate effectively, only a few employees can be on vacation at the same time. Which of the following is the MOST advisable approach in making up the schedule?

    8. ...

    A. Draw up a schedule assigning vacations in alphabetical order
    B. Find out when the supervisors want to take their vacations, and randomly assign whatever periods are left to the non-supervisory personnel
    C. Assign the most desirable times to employees of longest standing and the least desirable times to the newest employees
    D. Have all employees state their own preference, and then work out any conflicts in consultation with the people involved

9. Assume that you have been asked to prepare job descriptions for various positions in your department. Which of the following are the BASIC POINTS that should be covered in a *job description*?

    9. ...

    A. General duties and responsibilities of the position, with examples of day-to-day tasks
    B. Comments on the performances of present employees
    C. Estimates of the number of openings that may be available in each category during the coming year
    D. Instructions for carrying out the specific tasks assigned to your department

10. Of the following, the biggest DISADVANTAGE in allowing a free flow of communications in an agency is that such a free flow

    10. ...

    A. *decreases* creativity
    B. *increases* the use of the "grapevine"
    C. *lengthens* the chain of command
    D. *reduces* the executive's power to direct the flow of information

11. A downward flow of authority in an organization is one   11. ...
example of _____ communication .
     A. horizontal   B. informal   C. circular   D. vertical

12. Of the following, the one that would *most likely* block   12. ...
effective communication is
     A. concentration only on the issues at hand
     B. lack of interest or commitment
     C. use of written reports   D. use of charts and graphs

13. An ADVANTAGE of the *lecture* as a teaching tool is that it   13. ...
     A. enables a person to present his ideas to a large
        number of people
     B. allows the audience to retain a maximum of the infor-
        mation given
     C. holds the attention of the audience for the longest
        time
     D. enables the audience member to easily recall the main
        points

14. An ADVANTAGE of the *small-group* discussion as a teaching   14. ...
tool is that
     A. it always focuses attention on one person as the leader
     B. it places collective responsibility on the group as a
        whole
     C. its members gain experience by summarizing the ideas of
        others
     D. each member of the group acts as a member of a team

15. The one of the following that is an ADVANTAGE of a *large-*   15. ...
group discussion, when compared to a small-group discussion,
is that the large-group discussion
     A. moves along more quickly than a small-group discussion
     B. allows its participants to feel more at ease, and
        speak out more freely
     C. gives the whole group a chance to exchange ideas on a
        certain subject at the same occasion
     D. allows its members to feel a greater sense of personal
        responsibility

KEYS (CORRECT ANSWERS)

	TEST 1				TEST 2		
1. D		11. B	1. D	6. D		11. D	
2. A		12. C	2. C	7. B		12. B	
3. C		13. B	3. D	8. D		13. A	
4. D		14. A	4. D	9. A		14. D	
5. B		15. C	5. C	10. D		15. C	
6. B		16. A					
7. C		17. D					
8. D		18. A					
9. A		19. A					
10. A		20. B					
	21. D						
	22. B						
	23. B						
	24. A						
	25. B						

COMMUNICATION
EXAMINATION SECTION

DIRECTIONS FOR THIS SECTION:
    Each question or incomplete statement is followed by several sug-
gested answers or completions. Select the one that BEST answers the
question or completes the statement. *PRINT THE LETTER OF THE CORRECT
ANSWER IN THE SPACE AT THE RIGHT.*

TEST 1

1. In some agencies the counsel to the agency head is given   1. ...
   the right to bypass the chain of command and issue orders
   directly to the staff concerning matters that involve certain specific processes and practices.
   This situation *most nearly* illustrates the PRINCIPLE of
       A. the acceptance theory of authority
       B. multiple - linear authority
       C. splintered authority   D. functional authority
2. It is commonly understood that communication is an impor-   2. ...
   tant part of the administrative process.
   Which of the following is NOT a valid principle of the
   communication process in administration?
       A. The channels of communication should be spontaneous
       B. The lines of communication should be as direct and
          as short as possible
       C. Communications should be authenticated
       D. The persons serving in communications centers should
          be competent
3. Of the following, the *one* factor which is generally con-   3. ...
   sidered LEAST essential to successful committee operations
   is
       A. stating a clear definition of the authority and scope
          of the committee
       B. selecting the committee chairman carefully
       C. limiting the size of the committee to four persons
       D. limiting the subject matter to that which can be
          handled in group discussion
4. Of the following, the FAILURE by line managers to accept   4. ...
   and appreciate the benefits and limitations of a new program or system *very frequently* can be traced to the
       A. budgetary problems involved
       B. resultant need to reduce staff
       C. lack of controls it engenders
       D. failure of top management to support its implementation
5. If a manager were thinking about using a committee of sub-   5. ...
   ordinates to solve an operating problem, which of the following would generally NOT be an *advantage* of such use of
   the committee approach?
       A. Improved coordination   B. Low cost
       C. Increased motivation   D. Integrated judgment
6. Every supervisor has many occasions to lead a conference   6. ...
   or participate in a conference of some sort.
   Of the following statements that pertain to conferences
   and conference leadership, which is generally considered
   to be MOST valid?
       A. Since World War II, the trend has been toward fewer
          shared decisions and more conferences.

1

    B. The most important part of a conference leader's job
       is to direct discussion.
    C. In providing opportunities for group interaction,
       management should avoid consideration of its past
       management philosophy.
    D. A good administrator cannot lead a good conference
       if he is a poor public speaker.
7. Of the following, it is usually LEAST desirable for a   7. ...
   conference leader to
    A. call the name of a person after asking a question
    B. summarize proceedings periodically
    C. make a practice of repeating questions
    D. ask a question without indicating who is to reply
8. Assume that, in a certain organization, a situation has   8. ...
   developed in which there is little difference in status
   or authority between individuals.
   Which of the following would be the *most likely* result
   with regard to COMMUNICATION in this organization?
    A. Both the accuracy and flow of communication will be
       improved.
    B. Both the accuracy and flow of communication will sub-
       stantially decrease.
    C. Employees will seek more formal lines of communication.
    D. Neither the flow nor the accuracy of communication
       will be improved over the former hierarchical structure.
9. The main function of many agency administrative officers   9. ...
   is "information management." Information that is received
   by an administrative officer may be classified as active
   or passive, depending upon whether or not it requires the
   recipient to take some action.
   Of the following, the item received which is *clearly* the
   MOST active information is
    A. an appointment of a new staff member
    B. a payment voucher for a new desk
    C. a press release concerning a past event
    D. the minutes of a staff meeting
10. Of the following, the one LEAST considered to be a com-   10. ...
   munication barrier is
    A. group feedback   B. charged words
    C. selective perception   D. symbolic meanings
11. Management studies support the hypothesis that, in spite   11. ...
   of the tendency of employees to censor the information
   communicated to their supervisor, subordinates are *more
   likely* to communicate problem-oriented information UPWARD
   when they have a
    A. long period of service in the organization
    B. high degree of trust in the supervisor
    C. high educational level
    D. low status on the organizational ladder
12. Electronic data processing equipment can produce more in-   12. ...
   formation faster than can be generated by any other means.
   In view of this, the *most important* PROBLEM faced by management at present is to
    A. keep computers fully occupied
    B. find enough computer personnel
    C. assimilate and properly evaluate the information

D. obtain funds to establish appropriate information systems

13. A well-designed management information system *essentially*   13. ...
provides each executive and manager the INFORMATION he
needs for
    A. determining computer time requirements
    B. planning and measuring results
    C. drawing a new organization chart
    D. developing a new office layout

14. It is generally agreed that management policies should be   14. ...
periodically reappraised and restated in accordance with
current conditions.
Of the following, the approach which would be MOST effective in determining whether a policy should be revised is
to
    A. conduct interviews with staff members at all levels
       in order to ascertain the relationship between the
       policy and actual practice
    B. make proposed revisions in the policy and apply it
       to current problems
    C. make up hypothetical situations using both the old
       policy and a revised version in order to make compar-
       isons
    D. call a meeting of top level staff in order to discuss
       ways of revising the policy

15. Your superior has asked you to notify division employees   15. ...
of an important change in one of the operating procedures
described in the division manual. Every employee presently
has a copy of this manual.
Which of the following is normally the *most practical* way
to get the employees to UNDERSTAND such a change?
    A. Notify each employee individually of the change and
       answer any questions he might have
    B. Send a written notice to key personnel, directing
       them to inform the people under them
    C. Call a general meeting, distribute a corrected page
       for the manual, and discuss the change
    D. Send a memo to employees describing the change in
       general terms and asking them to make the necessary
       corrections in their copies of the manual

16. Assume that the work in your department involves the use   16. ...
of many technical terms.
In such a situation, when you are answering inquiries
from the general public, it would *usually* be BEST to
    A. use simple language and avoid the technical terms
    B. employ the technical terms whenever possible
    C. bandy technical terms freely, but explain each term
       in parentheses
    D. apologize if you are forced to use a technical term

17. Suppose that you receive a telephone call from someone   17. ...
identifying himself as an employee in another city department who asks to be given information which your own department regards as confidential.
Which of the following is the BEST way of handling such a
request?

3

A. Give the information requested, since your caller
   has official standing
B. Grant the request, provided the caller gives you a
   signed receipt
C. Refuse the request, because you have no way of knowing whether the caller is really who he claims to be
D. Explain that the information is confidential and inform the caller of the channels he must go through to
   have the information released to him

18. Studies show that office employees place high importance 18. ...
on the social and human aspects of the organization. What
office employees like best about their jobs is the kind of
people with whom they work. So strive hard to group people
who are most likely to get along well together.
Based on this information, it is *most reasonable* to assume
that office workers are MOST pleased to work in a group
which
   A. is congenial   B. has high productivity
   C. allows individual creativity
   D. is unlike other groups

19. A certain supervisor does not compliment members of his 19. ...
staff when they come up with good ideas. He feels that
coming up with good ideas is part of the job and does not
merit special attention.
This supervisor's practice is
   A. *poor*, because recognition for good ideas is a good
      motivator
   B. *poor*, because the staff will suspect that the super-
      visor has no good ideas of his own
   C. *good*, because it is reasonable to assume that employ-
      ees will tell their supervisor of ways to improve
      office practice
   D. *good*, because the other members of the staff are not
      made to seem inferior by comparison

20. Some employees of a department have sent an anonymous 20. ...
letter containing many complaints to the department head.
Of the following, what is this *most likely* to show about
the department?
   A. It is probably a good place to work.
   B. Communications are probably poor.
   C. The complaints are probably unjustified.
   D. These employees are probably untrustworthy.

21. Which of the following actions would usually be MOST AP- 21. ...
PROPRIATE for a supervisor to take *after* receiving an
instruction sheet from his superior explaining a new
procedure which is to be followed?
   A. Put the instruction sheet aside temporarily until he
      determines what is wrong with the old procedure
   B. Call his superior and ask whether the procedure is
      one he must implement immediately
   C. Write a memorandum to the superior asking for more
      details
   D. Try the new procedure and advise the superior of any
      problems or possible improvements

22. Of the following, which one is considered the PRIMARY ad- 22. ...
vantage of using a committee to resolve a problem in an
organization?

4

A. No one person will be held accountable for the decision since a group of people was involved
B. People with different backgrounds give attention to the problem
C. The decision will take considerable time so there is unlikely to be a decision that will later be regretted
D. One person cannot dominate the decision-making process

23. Employees in a certain office come to their supervisor   23. ...
with all their complaints about the office and the work. Almost every employee has had at least one minor complaint at some time.
The situation with respect to complaints in this office may BEST be described as *probably*
    A. *good;* employees who complain care about their jobs and work hard
    B. *good;* grievances brought out into the open can be corrected
    C. *bad;* only serious complaints should be discussed
    D. *bad;* it indicates the staff does not have confidence in the administration

24. The administrator who allows his staff to suggest ways to   24. ...
do their work will *usually* find that
    A. this practice contributes to high productivity
    B. the administrator's ideas produce greater output
    C. clerical employees suggest inefficient work methods
    D. subordinate employees resent performing a management function

25. The MAIN purpose for a supervisor's questioning the em-   25. ...
ployees at a conference he is holding is to
    A. stress those areas of information covered but not understood by the participants
    B. encourage participants to think through the problem under discussion
    C. catch those subordinates who are not paying attention
    D. permit the more knowledgeable participants to display their grasp of the problems being discussed

TEST 2

1. For a superior to use *consultative supervision* with his   1. ...
subordinates effectively, it is ESSENTIAL that he
    A. accept the fact that his formal authority will be weakened by the procedure
    B. admit that he does not know more than all his men together and that his ideas are not always best
    C. utilize a committee system so that the procedure is orderly
    D. make sure that all subordinates are consulted so that no one feels left out

2. The "grapevine" is an informal means of communication in   2. ...
an organization.
The attitude of a supervisor with respect to the grapevine should be to
    A. ignore it since it deals mainly with rumors and sensational information

    B. regard it as a serious danger which should be eliminated

    C. accept it as a real line of communication which should be listened to

    D. utilize it for most purposes instead of the official line of communication

3. The supervisor of an office that must deal with the public   3. ...
should realize that planning in this type of work situation

    A. is *useless* because he does not know how many people will request service or what service they will request

    B. *must be done at a higher level* but that he should be ready to implement the results of such planning

    C. is *useful* primarily for those activities that are not concerned with public contact

    D. is *useful* for all the activities of the office, including those that relate to public contact

4. Assume that it is your job to receive incoming telephone   4. ...
calls. Those calls which you cannot handle yourself have to be transferred to the appropriate office.
If you receive an outside call for an extension line which is busy, the one of the following which you should do FIRST is to

    A. interrupt the person speaking on the extension and tell him a call is waiting

    B. tell the caller the line is busy and let him know every thirty seconds whether or not it is free

    C. leave the caller on "hold" until the extension is free

    D. tell the caller the line is busy and ask him if he wishes to wait

5. Your superior has subscribed to several publications di-   5. ...
rectly related to your division's work, and he has asked you to see to it that the publications are circulated among the supervisory personnel in the division. There are eight supervisors involved.
The BEST method of insuring that all eight see these publications is to

    A. place the publication in the division's general reference library as soon as it arrives

    B. inform each supervisor whenever a publication arrives and remind all of them that they are responsible for reading it

    C. prepare a standard slip that can be stapled to each publication, listing the eight supervisors and saying, "Please read, initial your name, and pass along"

    D. send a memo to the eight supervisors saying that they may wish to purchase individual subscriptions in their own names if they are interested in seeing each issue

6. Your superior has telephoned a number of key officials in   6. ...
your agency to ask whether they can meet at a certain time next month. He has found that they can all make it, and he has asked you to confirm the meeting.
Which of the following is the BEST way to confirm such a meeting?

    A. Note the meeting on your superior's calendar

    B. Post a notice of the meeting on the agency bulletin board

    C. Call the officials on the day of the meeting to remind them of the meeting

    D. Write a memo to each official involved, repeating the time and place of the meeting

7. Assume that a new city regulation requires that certain   7. ...
   kinds of private organizations file information forms with
   your department. You have been asked to write the short
   explanatory message that will be printed on the front cover
   of the pamphlet containing the forms and instructions.
   Which of the following would be the MOST appropriate way
   of beginning this message?
   - A. Get the readers' attention by emphasizing immediately that there are legal penalties for organizations that fail to file before a certain date
   - B. Briefly state the nature of the enclosed forms and the types of organizations that must file
   - C. Say that your department is very sorry to have to put organizations to such an inconvenience
   - D. Quote the entire regulation adopted by the city, even if it is quite long and is expressed in complicated legal language

8. Suppose that you have been told to make up the vacation   8. ...
   schedule for the 18 employees in a particular unit. In
   order for the unit to operate effectively, only a few em-
   ployees can be on vacation at the same time.
   Which of the following is the MOST advisable approach in
   making up the schedule?
   - A. Draw up a schedule assigning vacations in alphabetical order
   - B. Find out when the supervisors want to take their vaca- tions, and randomly assign whatever periods are left to the non-supervisory personnel
   - C. Assign the most desirable times to employees of longest standing and the least desirable times to the newest employees
   - D. Have all employees state their own preference, and then work out any conflicts in consultation with the people involved

9. Assume that you have been asked to prepare job descriptions 9. ...
   for various positions in your department.
   Which of the following are the BASIC POINTS that should be
   covered in a *job description*?
   - A. General duties and responsibilities of the position, with examples of day-to-day tasks
   - B. Comments on the performances of present employees
   - C. Estimates of the number of openings that may be avail- able in each category during the coming year
   - D. Instructions for carrying out the specific tasks as- signed to your department

10. Of the following, the biggest DISADVANTAGE in allowing a   10. ...
    free flow of communications in an agency is that such a
    free flow
    - A. *decreases* creativity
    - B. *increases* the use of the "grapevine"
    - C. *lengthens* the chain of command
    - D. *reduces* the executive's power to direct the flow of information

11. A downward flow of authority in an organization is one   11. ...
    example of _____ communication .
       A. horizontal   B. informal   C. circular   D. vertical
12. Of the following, the one that would *most likely* block   12. ...
    effective communication is
       A. concentration only on the issues at hand
       B. lack of interest or commitment
       C. use of written reports   D. use of charts and graphs
13. An ADVANTAGE of the *lecture* as a teaching tool is that it   13. ...
       A. enables a person to present his ideas to a large
          number of people
       B. allows the audience to retain a maximum of the infor-
          mation given
       C. holds the attention of the audience for the longest
          time
       D. enables the audience member to easily recall the main
          points
14. An ADVANTAGE of the *small-group* discussion as a teaching   14. ...
    tool is that
       A. it always focuses attention on one person as the leader
       B. it places collective responsibility on the group as a
          whole
       C. its members gain experience by summarizing the ideas of
          others
       D. each member of the group acts as a member of a team
15. The one of the following that is an ADVANTAGE of a *large-*   15. ...
    group discussion, when compared to a small-group discussion,
    is that the large-group discussion
       A. moves along more quickly than a small-group discussion
       B. allows its participants to feel more at ease, and
          speak out more freely
       C. gives the whole group a chance to exchange ideas on a
          certain subject at the same occasion
       D. allows its members to feel a greater sense of personal
          responsibility

KEYS (CORRECT ANSWERS)

TEST 1				TEST 2		
1. D		11. B	1. D	6. D	11. D	
2. A		12. C	2. C	7. B	12. B	
3. C		13. B	3. D	8. D	13. A	
4. D		14. A	4. D	9. A	14. D	
5. B		15. C	5. C	10. D	15. C	
6. B		16. A				
7. C		17. D				
8. D		18. A				
9. A		19. A				
10. A		20. B				
	21. D					
	22. B					
	23. B					
	24. A					
	25. B					

TECHNIQUES OF DECISION MAKING

CONTENTS

TECHNIQUES OF DECISION MAKING

INSTRUCTIONAL
OBJECTIVES

1. Ability to define decision making.

2. Ability to learn the decision-making formula.

3. Ability to learn how to state problems simply and accurately.

4. Ability to determine the difference between a symptom and a cause.

5. Ability to determine which facts are most important to a decision.

6. Ability to be able to qualify information according to importance and subject classification.

7. Ability to learn to identify two or more alternative solutions for a problem.

8. Ability to develop an openness to creative ideas.

9. Ability to learn to weigh the consequences of alternative decisions.

10. Ability to select and justify the most appropriate decision.

CONTENT

INTRODUCTION

Every person, each day, is faced by numerous situations which require the making of many decisions throughout the course of the day. It is necessary to answer such questions as: *When do I get up in the morning? What clothes will I wear? What will I have for breakfast? Which route will I take to school?*

Working in the field of public service, an individual is constantly faced with a series of situations which require him to take some particular course of action. Many such actions may not require special decision making on his part, because his particular organization has provided ways for him to make these decisions rather automatically. For example, there are department policies, and standard ways of performing certain jobs. A person also has his own past experiences of success which enable him to easily make certain decisions for such things as: the hours he should work, his rate of pay, and the required forms which must be completed for certain kinds of activities. All of these things are handled rather automatically on the job, because people have methods of handling certain things in certain ways. These become habit. They fit within a regular pattern.

There are many situations faced by a decision maker where the consequences of his action are so minor that it doesn't really matter which way he decides to solve a given problem as long as it is resolved: for example, what pencil to choose; the color of the paper on a final report; the diverting of automobiles during a traffic jam.

However, there are also other situations where the way a manager or supervisor solves a problem has great impact on an organization. Sometimes a person doesn't have a chance to actually know what is right and what is wrong. Judgment might have no well established basis. The opportunity to select between two alternatives of equal value does not exist. The situation is not clearcut. It requires thought and careful judgment; it has far-reaching consequences on the organization-affecting the quality of service, costs, schedules, the relationships between people in a working unit. Appropriate action must be taken in such assorted areas as overtime, employee dismissal, grievances, types of equipment to purchase, ways to reduce waste. The effectiveness and efficiency of the decision-making process of one individual can have far-reaching impact on a public-service organization.

Good decisions allow individuals to control and monitor their operations. Bad ones can cause worse problems and hinder the effectiveness of an organization. Things just don't happen by chance. They are made to happen. They are arranged. They can quite often be developed over a period of time which has been required by the nature of the problem or activity.

1. WHAT IS DECISION MAKING?

Decision making involves a conscious choice or selection of one behavior alternative from a group of two or more behavior alternatives.

Thus, there are two basic elements in a decision-making process: one, the matter of conscious choice, and the other of alternatives. *To decide, then, really means to cut off, to come to a conclusion, to end.*

2. *A FORMULA FOR DECISION MAKING*

Decision-making is a skill that can be developed. One way in which it can be developed is through a formula, a procedure which provides a formal process or system involving the basic rules of decision-making. There are no born decision makers, but some people appear to act very efficiently on the basis of hunches. These people may never be seen with charts and graphs, or performing a lot of analytical tasks. However, they've probably developed their own way of sifting facts and of solving problems. Good decision makers usually know their personnel; have prior experience; they can put together difficult possibilities quickly. They have their own personal *formulas* of decision making.

An effective technique to help make decisions is through the aid of a formula –a kind of check-off list to help find answers to difficult situations, to resolve problems, to handle unique situations. Such a formula enables one to take advantage of his past experiences, to see the whole picture, and to utilize all the facts he can find which are applicable to the solution.

A decision-making formula worthy of our consideration has six steps:

- *Isolate* - State the apparent problem or situation with which you plan to deal.

- *Analyze* - Gather the facts.

- *Diagnose* - Organize and interpret the facts.

- *Prescribe procedures* - State the <u>real</u> problem or situation.

- *Implement procedures -* Develop alternative solutions.

- *Evaluate* - Select the most appropriate alternative. <u>Decide.</u>

We will consider each of these steps separately. However, it should be kept in mind that these separate steps are really all related and part of the whole process of decision making.

A. *Isolate the Problem*. A problem can be a situation, question, matter, or person that is perplexing or difficult, that obstructs the way to achieving a goal or objective.

Almost everyone has problems: students have study problems when they don't know answers to test questions; people have money problems when they can't pay all of their bills. Individuals have problems with people who are unfriendly; problems with their girlfriends or boyfriends; growth problems; health problems; psychological problems.

There are professionals and specialists to whom people can go with their problems. A person takes his malfunctioning car to a mechanic, he calls on the plumber to fix leaky pipes, contacts the doctor when he doesn't feel well. These specialists are skilled problem solvers in a particular area. They have had special training and experience. They may even have had to pass examinations to obtain certificates or licenses.

In decision making, one must recognize problems as well as symptoms of problems. It is particularly important to be able to separate symptoms from causes.

What is the Real Problem? Problems are often presented in very broad terms: "Gee, John, they've really fouled up in accounting. Go straighten them out." "Boy, do we have a morale problem." "We have to introduce that new system right away." "Those two managers just don't get along."

Consider the question of morale, for example. Is morale really the problem, or is it more accurately the symptom of another problem? Chances are that it is a symptom of a problem rather than the real problem itself. The problem situation might be poor organizational structure, bad working conditions, an unfriendly supervisor, unfair treatment, or a number of other difficulties.

To help in determining what is a symptom and what is a cause, several questions must be asked:

- *"How else might the problem be stated?"* The placement of accountants in one isolated department, without the opportunity to discuss actual income and outgo with supervisors, has given us unrealistic budget figures.

  The lack of adding machines, a broken calculator, dim light, uncomfortable room temperatures, and individual working spaces has caused a greater number of absences.

  The accounting manager has openly criticized senior staff members in front of their fellow workers.

  The department secretaries were all forced to work overtime for staying five minutes past their lunch hours.

- *"What else is involved?"*

  If there are no communications between accountants and supervisors, neither group will know the reasons behind the requests or needs of the others.

  There has been talk about a computer eliminating some of the accounting jobs.

  The senior accountants have been slow to pick up the new accounting procedures.

  This is the tenth time this month that the financial unit has been unable to take care of the people in line because the secretaries were not here.

- *"Are there similar problems in other departments?"*

  The people in supplies have been ordering the wrong equipment.

  There have been layoffs in several departments.

  Several department managers are competing for the job of assistant director of our organization.

  None of the other departments have problems with secretaries.

○ *"Is this a problem or a symptom?"*

The real problem is that the accountants have not been properly informed of the organizational structure, and thus have very poor understanding of the departments which comprise the organization.

Another organization nearby has announced opportunities for accountants at higher pay, and in new offices.

The accounting manager and his senior staff do not plan departmental modifications together.

Only one of the secretaries has a watch and it is five minutes slow. They play bridge at lunch time several days each month.

○ *"How do others perceive the problem?"*

Talk to all the accountants and managers individually.

Talk to personnel about accounting re-classification.

Interview the senior staff.

Visit with the secretaries.

What are the Problems? What are the Symptoms? If your automobile won't start, it might not be because it's old, the engine is dirty, or your windshield wipers don't work the car may be out of gas. It might, however, be time to give it some other attention, too. If you can recognize the symptoms, you can avoid a lot of problems.

B. Analyze the Facts. When the problem is recognized, then all the facts required for a successful decision can, and should be accumulated. Too often, people think they have all the facts, but they don't. It's like trying to put together a jigsaw puzzle, and recognizing, after many frustrating hours, that six pieces are missing.

Frequently, the decision maker feels that because he is in a particular situation, he knows it better than anyone else can know it. The issue may, therefore, be somewhat clouded. This cloudiness may prevent him from seeing what is actually there.

How many times have individuals had to make a decision and found that they didn't have the right facts or sufficient quantities of facts to insure a good decision? Both the quality and effectiveness of most decisions can be seriously reduced without good facts.

When gathering facts, one should write them down, and gather them into one comprehensive list. The decision maker can then visualize them all at the same time, and is much less likely to overlook or forget any of them. In dealing with large amounts of information, he can grade sub-topics and keep track of them in a systematic way.

How many facts should be gathered? The number usually depends on the nature and complexity of the situation.

Basically it means that the amount of information accumulated depends upon such factors as:

○ The amount of time available.

○ Is it an emergency situation or not?

○ The seriousness of the situation.

○ The availability of information, etc.

Where are the Needed Facts Obtained?

○ First, he might turn to available records. He usually has financial records, personal records, records of transactions, and records of activities.

○ Second, he may have references: newspapers, journals, old letters, the like.

○ Third, and very importantly, he has other people, or he has a staff. There is a great deal of expertise within most public-service organizations: specialists in economics, human relations, law, health, safety, and other areas; all responsive to the request of the decision-maker. An outside expert, or consultant, may be required in difficult situations.

○ Finally, look at other organizational units which have been confronted with similar problems. Quite often, through investigation, the decision-maker finds that precedents have been set which he may have to follow. In law, for example, he may have to base a decis.ion on the verdict of a case held on the same issue, long ago in a distant place.

Sources of information are unlimited. It takes a great deal of initiative to uncover them.

How should the facts be obtained? Here again, there are questions we must ask ourselves:

○ What kinds of facts are available?

○ What information is available?

○ Is there enough?

- Is help needed, and where can it be obtained?

- Who else might have the information needed?

Going back to the morale problem, which was found to be the result of a basic lack of communication between accountants and departmental managers, how might the decision-maker proceed?

In gathering the facts, he would have to obtain both the accountant's records and the manager's records. The decision-maker might call upon organizations of similar size and activity, to see how they handle difficulties of this nature. He might talk to one or more senior accountants in a large public accounting firm or contact the governmental auditors. He might even write letters to colleagues seeking their advice.

The decision-maker might hold a meeting of selected members of his staff, or assign a task force of accountants and managers to look into the matter.

As he begins to gather his facts, the decision-maker will discover that other information is required. Additionally, he will uncover sources of other facts. The quality of the facts he gathers ultimately affects the quality of his decisions. The better the data, the better the opportunity to make a good decision.

C. Organizing the Facts. Once the facts have been collected, it becomes very important that they be organized to help the decision-maker interpret what they really mean. To do this, it's helpful to set them up in categories -- to pull like items together.

This procedure helps people to know whether certain facts are more important than others, and thus deserve special consideration.

Grouping the Facts. There are several categories into which information can be grouped, such as: cost, time, past precedent, procedures, leadership, quality, and productivity:

Cost.   In cost considerations, one must look at unit costs, personnel costs, material costs, equipment costs, mailing costs, etc. If, for example, an individual is attempting to determine the cost of mailing out new contracts to several hundred vendors with whom the agency deals, the following costs may have to be considered, among others:

- *Duplication costs per duplicated copy.*

- *Salary costs of writing new contract.*

- *Salary costs of typing contracts.*

- *Costs of new contract forms.*

o   *Costs of envelopes.*

o   *Costs of writing departmental letters.*

Time.   Time is usually calculated in terms of the personnel costs or salaries paid. The basic periods of time hours, days, weeks, months, years are quite often combined in terms of man-hours, man-weeks, man-years, etc., to enable the numbers of hour units to be multiplied by salary allocations. Equipment time, particularly in this age of computers, can be quite expensive.

Past Precedent.   This is a category relating together data on similar situations in the past, and to consider the decisions arrived at in those situations for their bearing on the decision to be made in the present.

Procedures.   These are also important. Most public-service organizations have certain ways of accomplishing functions or providing services. They have been proven over a period of time to be most appropriate to particular situations. Here, too, is where organizational policy making may be involved and possibly changed and modified.

Leadership. This would include the directions and decisions which brought about a particular situation, and permit review of the factors which were present when prior decisions were made.

Quality. The quality of facts is important. There must be an assurance that the right data, and the most applicable figures and information, are available.

Productivity. This category would enable a comparison between various activities which would bring about particular results. It would provide an opportunity to look at the output of a department or project team.

In pulling together like items, one can see trends, certain facts which may be more important than others, and areas where there are gaps in the information.

In organizing facts, the following questions should be asked:

o   Which facts are related to each other?

o   Are these facts related to any not listed?

o   What is the extent of their relationship?

o   Are they relevant to this situation?

o   What is the level of reliability of the facts?

o   Can the problem be more clearly defined with the information listed?

- How can it be done?

- How much time is there for further organization?

- Are these facts recurring or one time events?

D. *Stating the Real Problem*. Having examined the data, the decision-maker is now in a position to state the *real* problem or situation with which he has to deal. He now knows whether he has a problem, or just a misunderstanding. Was the original statement just a symptom, or was it a real situation? It might be that there are several problems. Whatever the situation, it must be stated in clear and simple terms. It should be written down.

A problem is a situation which deviates from an expected standard, or norm of desired performance. In decision making, one starts with an *apparent* problem. The decision maker gathers more information in order to more accurately identify the situation with which he is going to deal.

Is there a real problem? or just symptoms? The data have been gathered and organized. Now it is necessary to zero in on the actual situation, and to see whether there is a real problem. Was the initial identification a symptom of a problem, or was it a real cause? Is there one problem, or several?

If the decision-maker neglected to gather the facts, and then to organize, analyze, and categorize them, he might find himself working on the wrong situation. He could spend a great deal of time and effort on symptoms, and could actually be working on the wrong problem. Certainly, he could over-look a number of relevant factors.

If a medical doctor spent all of his time studying symptoms, he might be too late to address an actual problem and his patient could die. Similarly, in a public-service organization, *if too much time and energy is spent in chasing symptoms instead of causes, problems can become crises.*

What objective is to be achieved? Remember, one must still think about decision making in terms of fulfilling objectives.

When it is known what kind of performance should be achieved, and what kind of performance has been received, the necessary effort is simple merely to measure the difference between those two points. The decision-maker must identify the deviation and its extent. He will also have to specifi-cally state the standard, or *norm,* toward which he is trying to return.

In other words, not only does he have to state the problem to which he is going to address himself, but he must specifically state the objective he wants to achieve.

In the previous illustration of the public-service organization and the commu-nication problems between the accountants and managers, the objectives could, perhaps, be restated in this manner: *it is necessary to design a realistic and accurate budget for costs.*

This stage would complete the problem identification part of the decision-making process. Now, he can get on with decision-making itself.

E.   *Developing Alternative Solutions.* With the *real* problem determined and stated, the decision-maker is now in a position to begin the development of alternative solutions. Notice that there is an "s" on the end of "solution." Decision-makers should be interested in as many solutions to a problem as can be developed.

This particular phase of the decision making process should be very free-wheeling. It should produce a number of ideas. The decision-maker should keep his mind open. He should not be too judgmental, but should avoid premature criticism. *Criticism given too early can destroy new ideas that could be beneficial.*

Picture a staff meeting, where the assistant director of the agency presents an entirely new approach to providing recreational opportunities for senior citizens. He is interrupted by his superior, the director, who tells him that his idea is ridiculous. It is unlikely that he would ever bring up the subject again unless he were extremely persistent and unafraid of the director. *Creative thinking can be squelched by a superior who criticizes without having much of a basis for criticism.*

The number of alternatives that can be developed at any one point in time is a function of how much time is spent in developing these alternatives. It's always helpful to stop and ask: "If I didn't have any rules to follow in this organization, would I handle the situation any differently?" Or, "What else could I do?" Perhaps it is desirable to modify several previously stated alternatives to produce one better alternative.

Present all alternatives for consideration. By considering all ideas as initially feasible, they can be brought out into the open. Such occasions are often called brain storming sessions. Regardless of how silly an idea might seem at first, perhaps when it is considered in the light of other possibilities it may turn out to be a fairly useable solution; or maybe a portion of that idea might be able to be combined with another idea and thereby produce the ultimate solution.

What, for example, would have happened if someone stifled the idea of the paper clip? "Isn't that stupid, who'd want to hold pieces of paper together with bent up wire?" Evidently, people laughed at Columbus, and his idea of a round world; they laughed at John Fulton and his steamship; and even at a young man named Fosbury, who high-jumped backwards. Regardless of ridicule, however, each of these men, in his solution to the problem at hand, succeeded in his particular project.

How many people have been shot-down in creative projects, by comments such as these: "We've tried it and it didn't work," "That's against policy," "It would cost too much," "He hasn't got the experience," "He"'s too young."

List the Alternatives. Looking at the positive side of the argument, there should be positive consideration of all methods, objects, and persons available, to satisfy the needs of decision-making. Once again, write down all of the alternatives, so that they can be comprehensively considered.

To do this, one can list all of the alternatives across the top of a chart and then systematically consider all the factors under each alternative. This chart, or *matrix,* as it is called, can then be used to evaluate the best solution.

As an example, let us assume legislation is passed in each state to award home and business loans and educational benefits to veterans of the Vietnam war. Then a matrix somewhat like this can be made:

	ALTERNATIVES				
	#1	#2	#3	#4	#5
Staff involved					
Labor costs					
Material costs					
Equipment costs					
Services included					
Services excluded					
facilities needed					
Number of veterans processed per day					
Publicity requirements					
Applicable policy					
New policies needed,					
etc.					

The list can be long, but it is well worth it. If, for example, one is considering attending a community college or university, but can't make up his mind. He can develop a chart with all of the things that are important to him on the side of the chart, and the schools under consideration acros the top. Then a five-point scale can *be* applied to each item, with five being the highest mark and zero the lowest. The school with the most points might be the most likely alternative under all the prevailing circumstances. Still, one cannot be completely definite on this basis alone, so it is necessary to move to the next step in the decision-making process, that of selection.

F. Selecting the Best Alternative Solution. The most important part of the decision-making process is the selection of the most appropriate alternative: *deciding.* This is the stage during which criticism is appropriate. Judgment must be made on all facets of the problem and the alternative solutions. The effectiveness of each of the solutions must be evaluated in terms of the objectives towards which the decision-maker is oriented. He must look carefully at, and criticize severely, such items as cost, timeliness, workability, acceptability, and implementation.

- Can the solution be made to work?

- Will the staff cooperate?

- Will those who are served make the necessary adjustments?

- Are there the skills in the organization to carry out the program?

List the Consequences of the Decision. As these and other items are considered, it is desirable to write down <u>all</u> of the consequences of <u>each</u> of the decisions. List the pro's and con's. It is not enough to add them together and make a decision on that basis, such as in the selection of a college, in the previous section. Not only does one use some type of scale, but he assigns different weights to different items. Using the previous college selection chart, the decision-maker might have to weight costs higher than the availability of co-educational dormitories, or the scholastic reputation of the school over the strength of its football team.

Be a Devil's Advocate. The more desirable alternatives should be scrutinized in a negative way. Take the opposite position, that is, play the *devil's advocate.* Mentally implement the plan and consider the adverse consequences.

Take one of the most favorable-looking alternatives. Ask:

- "Will it affect other departments?"

- "What could go wrong?"

- "What are the potential sources of breakdown?"

- "What new problem might it create?"

- "Where would the resistance be?"

Consider the extent to which these consequences will probably come about and the degree of seriousness of each one. Select second and even third choices in order to plan for contingencies.

Scrutinize the Final Alternative Thoroughly . Once the alternatives have been narrowed to only one, which appears to fill the need, then this one alternative should be subjected to one final round of positive questions:

- ○ Will this decision fulfill the original goal?

- ○ Can the agency live with the decision permanently?

- ○ Is the timing of the decision right?

- ○ Does the decision bring about the greatest benefit for the greatest number?

Involve Your Superiors. It is often necessary and desirable to go to the superiors with the decision. Ordinarily, the problem would be presented, with the attendant factors affecting it, and the alternative solutions which could resolve it. Then the decision-maker would indicate his reasons, with their consequences, for selection of the particular alternative.

G. Implement the Decision. After a decision is made, it must be implemented. The necessary steps must be initiated to carry it out. The whole management cycle of planning, organizing, and controlling must be brought into action, as well as other available management tools.

3. SUMMATION

No phase of the management cycle or any other organizational function could be carried out if decisions were not made. Planning, organizing, controlling, as well as motivating, communicating, and setting standards; these all require endless strings of decisions or choices. This is why the final process of decision making is so important.

Good decisions are the result of understanding responsibilities, involving others, knowing the organization, understanding one's own strengths and weaknesses, and being accountable for decisions made.

In understanding the responsibilities involved, one must know where to get information and be cognizant of the extent to which people can take action.

Through involving others, they gain a sense of ownership in the decision, and become more committed. They remove their defense mechanisms.

Knowing an organization requires an awareness of its organizational history and objectives, where the power centers lie, the limits of one's authority, and the way in which work is actually accomplished.

One's understanding of himself and his own shortcomings insures that he will seek out expertise he does not possess himself, and will develop ways to improve his own skills.

The individual should have this motto: *Remember, when you get right down to it, one person may have to decide – YOU!*

STUDENT
LEARNING
ACTIVITIES

o   Prepare a definition of *decision making,*

o   Write a brief paper on the decision-making formula.

o   Participate in a class discussion about decision making in a selected public-service agency. Try to identify top, middle, and low-level decisions.

o   Prepare a definition of the term *problem.*

o   Interview a public-service official to identify a problem within his organization. Follow with a class discussion.

o   Prepare a brief paper describing three examples of symptoms and their causes.

o   Participate in a problem-solving case study.

o   Write a brief paper on why facts must be gathered to aid in the decision-making process.

o   Identify the kinds of facts and resources you must use to prepare for making decisions about a teacher-assigned topic.

o   Participate in a discussion about fact finding.

o   Develop with the class, and have at least 20 students complete, a survey questionnaire with open-ended questions on ways in which your school can be improved. Organize responses according to subject and year ranking of importance.

o   Participate in a class discussion on the results of the questionnaire survey.

o   After the class has decided on one or more ways in which the school can be improved, prepare a report on one of the objectives including:

> statement of an objective,
>
> facts needed and how obtained,
>
> categorizing the facts.

o   Deliver an oral version of your report. Respond to questions and comments from the class,

o   Choose five articles from the newspaper on five different topics: sports, politics, crime, etc. State the actual problem being addressed.

○ Participate in a class discussion about problem identification, and problem statements. Sharpen your problem statements if necessary.

○ Participate in a class discussion about problems identified and possible alternative solutions.

○ Using the example of the State legislature passing a bill awarding home and business loans and educational benefits to veterans of the Gulf War, develop a set of alternative plans as to how the legislation may be carried out.

TEACHER MANAGEMENT ACTIVITIES

○ Have students define *decision making*.

○ Assign students a paper on the decision-making formula.

○ Conduct a class discussion about decision-making in a selected public service agency.

○ Have students prepare their own definitions of the term *problem*.

○ Assign students interviews with public-service officials to identify selected organizational problems.

○ Conduct a class discussion on problems in public-service organizations.

○ Have students develop and discuss reports and three examples of symptoms and their causes.

○ Select and assign a case study to the class in problem solving.

○ Assign a paper on why facts must be gathered to aid in the decision-making process.

○ Prepare a list of considerations in several public-service agencies. Have each student select one consideration around which he will gather essential facts to make a decision.

○ Conduct a discussion on fact finding.

○ Assign the class a survey project, entitled "How Can Our School be Improved?" Have students develop their own questionnaire and administer it to at least 20 students. Ask them to organize their results according to subject and rank of importance.

○ Organize a class discussion on the results of the surveys.

○ Once one or more items of possible school improvement have been agreed upon, assign the students a report to contain the following:

statement of an objective,

facts needed and how obtained,

categorizing of facts.

- ○   Organize oral presentations of student reports.

- ○   Assign students the reading of five articles from a newspaper on five different topics: sports, polttfcs, crime, etc. Have them state the actual problem being discussed.

- ○   Conduct a class discussion on problem identification and problem statements.

- ○   Assign a brief paper on the symptoms of five problems and the causes in a public service agency selected by each student.

- ○   Conduct a class discussion on the problems and solutions identified.

- ○   Using the example of the new bill for veterans of the Gulf War, have students develop a set of alternatives.

- ○   Insure that the students are open to new and abstract suggestions.

- ○   Direct oral presentations of students in which they review their original problems, the sources and categories of facts, the alternatives available for solution, their respective consequences, and their ultimate decisions. Have students challenge one another's decisions.

———

Evaluation Questions
Techniques of Decision Making

Read the problem carefully, and answer each of the following questions.

You are a library assistant. Mrs. Smith, the librarian, has two high school aides, Susan and Mary. Mrs. Smith has told you that she may fire Susan if her attitude does not improve. She complained about Susan's laziness and stated that Susan's work was never finished. Mrs. Smith asked you to talk to Susan about improving her attitude. When you tried to talk to Susan about this, she got upset and went home.

After observing the aides' workload for a few days, you notice that Susan has much more work than Mary.

1. What is the problem? _____
   _____
   _____
   _____

2. Name one solution. _____
   _____
   _____
   _____

3. What are the consequences of this solution? _____
   _____
   _____
   _____

4. List another solution. _____
   _____
   _____
   _____

5. What are the consequences of this solution? _____
   _____
   _____
   _____

6. Which do you think is the best solution? _____
   _____
   _____
   _____

Read the problem carefully, and answer each of the following questions.

You are in charge of the recreation program at the community center. Your job is to keep activities running smoothly. On the daily schedule, one-half hour has been set aside for basketball. While you have stepped out for a moment, ten of the Green Hornets and ten of the Purple Dragons arrived to play basketball. As each group has two teams set up, neither group would give in. Unfortunately, a fight began. The fight ended just as you returned. Each group plans to play tomorrow. You must make a decision.

1. What is the problem? _____
   _____
   _____
   _____

2. Name one solution. _____
   _____
   _____
   _____

3. What are the consequences of this solution?_____
   _____
   _____
   _____

4. List another solution. _____
   _____
   _____
   _____

5. What are the consequences of this solution?_____
   _____
   _____
   _____

6. Which do you think is the best solution? _____
   _____
   _____
   _____

Answer Key

Answers will vary on this test. The instructor may wish to have a discussion after the test, with students justifying their selections. Students may be evaluated on the soundness of their judgement.

BASIC FUNDAMENTALS OF ORAL COMMUNICATION

TABLE OF CONTENTS

BASIC FUNDAMENTALS OF
ORAL COMMUNICATION

Instructional Objectives

1. Ability to speak fluently, with correct articulation and pronunciation;
2. Ability to group words into meaningful phrases;
3. Ability to stress words and phrases to enhance communication;
4. Ability to control voice volume and tone according to needs;
5. Ability to use speech forms appropriate for the audience;
6. Ability to use body control and visual aids to enhance communication;
7. Ability to participate effectively in informal conversation and group discussion;
8. Ability to speak effectively and confidently before a group;
9. Ability to persuade or convince listeners; and
10. Ability to value the importance of oral communication as an essential skill for working in public service occupations.

Content

Introduction

Oral communication is one of the more basic processes underlying human relationships. The use of speech to transmit ideas, to probe the ideas of others, to teach, to persuade, to entertain, to motivate, and to otherwise influence and affect others is a uniquely human activity. Speech is used in the most casual and informal of human interactions, as well as in formal settings involving many persons. Through the mass media, the sounds and forms of speech may reach millions of persons simultaneously. Thus the ability to speak effectively in a variety of settings is an essential skill in all activities in which human beings interact with one another.

A basis is provided herein for the development of the student's ability to communicate effectively through speech for a variety of purposes and in a variety of settings, particularly those common to public-service occupational settings. Whatever the particular purpose or setting, however, effective speech will require the speaker to have a clear idea of his purpose and his audience, to organize his thoughts and information in an orderly way, to express himself effectively through his delivery and his knowledge of human relations, to report relevant facts, to explain and summarize clearly, and to evaluate the effectiveness of his communication.

This unit provides a framework for organizing instruction in basic speech skills, while providing practice in speaking for several purposes in several settings.

General Principles

Whatever the particular purpose or setting for oral communication, the speaker can add to his effectiveness by applying certain general principles. In general, these principles can be considered under two broad categories:

- principles affecting delivery, and
- principles affecting human relations.

These two categories are perhaps the most important aspects of oral communication. The principles of delivery and human relations must be applied in a variety of speaking situations.

Principles Affecting Delivery

The delivery of oral communications may be considered under two general categories of:

- *physical delivery,* which includes voice control, articulation, pronunciation, body control, and visual aids; and
- *verbal delivery,* including choice of words and style of delivery.

Physical Delivery

Voice Control: The effectiveness of oral communication depends in large measure upon the physical delivery of speech symbols, one major aspect which is voice control. Voice control has several distinguishing characteristics: pitch, volume, duration, and quality:

- *Pitch* is the characteristic of sound as it relates to the musical scale. Each person's voice has a certain pitch level that may be considered as high, low, or medium. Certain conditions of pitch can cause communication to suffer:
  - when the voice is pitched too high
  - when it is pitched too low
  - when it lacks variety of pitch and is monotonous

- *Volume,* or loudness, is another characteristic of voice. Speakers may be troubled when the voice volume is:
  - too great
  - too weak, or
  - lacking variety, or monotonous.

- *Duration* refers to the length of time a sound lasts, particularly the vowel sounds. There are two chief problems related to this control:
  - over-lengthening of vowels, resulting in a drawl
  - eliminating or clipping of vowels, resulting in erratic and staccato speech patterns.

- *Quality of voice* refers to that characteristic which distinguishes one person's voice from another's, the voice's "fingerprint," so to speak. The student should strive to achieve a pleasing and harmonious quality. Common quality faults include:
  - nasality (too much nasal resonance)
  - denasality (too little nasal resonance)
  - harshness, hoarseness and breathiness.

Articulation: To make himself understood, the speaker must produce speech in such a way that the audience is able to recognize the individual words he speaks. This is dependent upon the elements of:

- *Articulation,* or the joining together of consonants and vowels that go to make up the word, and

2

- *pronunciation,* or the fitting together of these sounds according to commonly accepted standards.

These concepts are often confused. *Articulation has to do with the clarity or distinctness of utterance,* while *pronunciation has to do with regional or dictionary standards.* It may be said, "We mispronounce words when we don't know how to pronounce them; we misarticulate words when we know how to pronounce them but fail to do so." Through habit, carelessness, and indifference, individuals may acquire such articulation problems as:
- *substitution of one sound for another,* in such words as:
    - "dat" for that
    - "winduh" for window
    - "git" for get
    - "yur" for your
    - "liddle" for little

- *insertion of extra sounds,* as:
    - ath-uh-lete for athlete
    - ekscape for escape
    - acrosst for across
    - fil-um for film.

- *omission of certain sounds,* such as:
    - at for that
    - probly for probably
    - em for them
    - slep for slept
    - pitcher for picture

- *misplacement of accent,* for example:
    - com-PAIR-a-ble for COM-par-a-ble
    - pre-FER-a-ble for PREF-er-a-ble
    - the-A-ter for THE-a-ter

Pronunciation: A person may be able to form all the speech sounds in a word accurately without saying the word correctly. The letters of words do not always represent the same sounds. When the person can form the sounds of a word correctly but does not know the acceptable way to form them, he has a pronunciation problem. The way to achieve acceptable pronunciation is to check new words in the dictionary and to be sensitive to the pronunciations heard in the speech of others. If others pronounce a word differently, the word should be looked up at the very next opportunity before using it again. The teacher must play a central role in identifying words misarticulated and mispronounced by students.

Body Language as Communication: In addition to voice and articulation-pronunciation controls, a speaker's whole body acts as an important tool in the physical delivery of speech. Through the judicious use of eye contact, facial expression, and body activity the speaker can supplement and reinforce his spoken communication by means of visual symbols.

Eye Contact: It is important for effective oral communication that the listeners feel that the speaker is speaking directly to them. No matter if the speaker is addressing one person or many, each listener should gain a feeling that the speaker is addressing him. Thus, *eye contact* between the speaker and his audience is essential in virtually every speaking situation. No matter what the setting, therefore, the speaker should make every attempt to meet the eyes of all members of the audience to achieve a feeling of directness and all-inclusiveness. The eyes of the speaker should meet those of members of the audience, not look past them or avoid them, nor over their heads, out of the window, down at the floor, or up at the ceiling. Eye contact with members of the audience will also help the speaker watch for audience reactions, for signs of misunderstanding, doubt, or question which may help him modify his communication in response to audience reactions.

Facial Expression: Another form of body control is the use of *facial expression* to clarify and enliven oral communication. The speaker's face, used effectively, can reflect his interest in his own message, the intensity of his feelings, his sincerity and purposefulness. Hiding behind a mask of blankness and composure can deny the speaker an important tool in the communication of his ideas. To develop this facility with facial expression, the learner should try always to communicate ideas in which he has a high interest and in which he has a sense of competence and concern. It is difficult to generate facial liveliness when speaking on a topic of little personal concern.

Body Activity: The use of gestures and general *body activity* provides another means for supplementing speech. The use of motor activity involving the head, torso, arms, hands, or gross body movement to emphasize the spoken word is a skill that may be cultivated. A shrug of the shoulders, a nod of the head, a straightening of the torso, a lift of the chin, or a step toward the audience can indicate indifference, emphasis, firmness of purpose, a questioning attitude, or determination.

Body activity can, however, be overdone to the point where too much activity may distract from the message. The use of body activity must be judicious if it is to have a controlled and desired effect on the listeners.

Another fault in this area involves the unconscious use of distracting mannerisms that may result from habit, nervousness, or preoccupation. Such mannerisms usually are unrelated to the content of the message, such as shifting weight from foot to foot, finger or foot tapping, nose or head fiddling, generalized arm waving, lint picking, and the like. The student should learn to normally use body movement only for specific purposes, while trying to eliminate all mannerisms and overuses that distract from the message.

Visual Aids Help Oral Communication: The physical delivery of speech may be enhanced also through the use of visual aids. Visual aids may be useful for several purposes:

- *for getting attention and interest.* Well-chosen and relevant aids command attention through their shape, color, texture, or movement. A speaker can capture attention by using materials that appeal directly to the senses.
- *for clarifying.* When words are insufficient to communicate an idea, a visual aid may help make an idea clearer. A sketch or drawing, a photograph or model, often can clarify in an instant what may be impossible to describe verbally.

4

- *for impressing on memory.* Aside from getting attention and clarifying an idea, the speaker may wish to affect the listener's memory. A well-chosen visual aid may help etch an idea on the memory far more effectively than a well-turned phrase.
- *for increasing poise.* The use of visual aids may provide a framework for the speaker's activity, giving him something to do that may serve to increase confidence. The use of visual aids as a "crutch" should not be encouraged in the long run; however, their use in this way may serve to aid the self-confidence of the learner in the initial stages of speech training.

Many types of visual aids may be found useful to supplement oral communications. These include charts, graphs, maps, globes, chalkboard sketches, flip charts, models, moving pictures, projected slides and illustrations, photographs, or television enlargements. In using visual aids, the speaker should follow several basic guidelines:
- He should use the visual material purposefully;
- He should be certain that the entire audience can see the aid;
- He should maintain eye contact while using the aid; and
- He should avoid dividing attention with the aid when it is not in use.

Verbal Delivery
The effectiveness of oral communication depends also upon the speaker's choice of language and his style of delivery. The words he uses, the phrasing by which he assembles them, and the manner in which he delivers them, are the elements of *verbal delivery.*

Choice of Language: Good language in oral communication is language adapted to the audience and to the occasion. In choosing language, the speaker must consider himself, the ideas he wants to express, the characteristics of the audience, and the nature of the setting. Thus he must ask himself, "Is this expression suitable for me to use in communicating this thought to this audience on this occasion?"

Use clear language: To accomplish this, the speaker should use language that clarifies his thoughts. Language should be simple and not pompous. Unnecessarily complex expressions or technical terms should be avoided. Too many words, too ornate words, too pretentious words, can hamper communication. The criteria of clarity in speaking are directness, economy, and aptness. For example,
- Instead of "prevarication", say "lie";
- Instead of "domicile", say "home";
- Instead of "this moment is one of great joy to my heart," say "I'm glad to be here."

Seek precise words: It is also a good idea to use precise language. Words and expressions which are specific to the intended meaning are more likely to communicate that meaning than more general and abstract words. In this vein:
- Instead of "car," try hardtop, sedan, Ford, or 1973 hatch-back Pinto;
- Instead of "said," try replied, stated, cried, commented, uttered.

Avoid imprecise wording: Avoid roundabout expressions, or *euphemisms,* which create special problems in lack of precision. "Soft-pedaling" an idea now and then may be justified if the speaker does not sacrifice his overall credibility. But care must be taken that the use of euphemisms does not act to call into question the speaker's ideas or intent. Therefore,

- Instead of "he passed to his just reward," try → "he died"
- "he received his termination notice" → "he was fired"
- "the effects were not inconsiderable" → "the effects were great"

Use appealing language: The speaker should also seek to use language that will enliven his thoughts. One way to achieve this is to use language that appeals to the senses. Thus language that appeals to movement, color, light, texture, form, taste, smell, sound, and the like will tend to put life in the speaking. Thus,

- Instead of "a difficult peace", try → "a hard and bitter peace"
- "an old ship" → "a splintery, creaking old ship"

Animate abstract ideas: Figurative language, too, can enliven speech by animating an abstract idea. The use of simile, metaphor, personification, and irony (look up the meanings in your dictionary) are especially useful. For example,

- Instead of "her arrival silenced everyone", try → "her arrival was like a chill winter wind"
- "he paced to and fro" → "he was like a caged lion"
- "the winds rustled the trees" → "the trees whispered in the winds"
- "we worked a lot of overtime" → "oh, we twiddled away our time and often left early!"

Use varied techniques: The speaker should develop ways to vary his choice of language. Variety in expression can help to sustain interest and attention, while often clarifying meaning. Students should practice changing their language by use of techniques such as:

- varying the shaping of sentences (use of questions, use of imperatives, varying order of phrases, etc.);
- building climax within passages;
- using parallelisms (recurring similarities of phrase or word arrangements);
- using alliteration (repeating first syllables, or consonants in consecutive words)
- using repetition of phraseology;
- using fresh language, i.e. avoiding the ordinary and the hackneyed, or shopworn, cliché-type phrases.

Use appropriate language: The speaker should always take special pains to use language appropriate to the occasion, and language which is standard. The speaker can be too formal or too informal, either of which will reduce, for particular occasions, the effectiveness of his communication. While the formality of language may be adjusted to the occasion, rarely will it be appropriate to use common slang or the language of the streets in any formal communication setting. Similarly, the use of standard speech will usually be appropriate and aid in communicating ideas, whereas the use of substandard language forms may inhibit understanding and reduce the speaker's credibility among many segments of his audience.

Use natural language: Further, it is important on all occasions that the speaker use language that is his own, language that is familiar and comfortable. Each student should work toward developing broader vocabulary and a greater variety of language skills, but should be discouraged from trying to achieve these in large steps. Language skills are developed over long periods of time, and at any given stage of development the student should use the language with which he is most comfortable and natural. In this way each student, over time, may develop uniqueness and effectiveness of style – that characteristic of one's speech which brands it distinctly as his own.

Develop a Good Style of Delivery: Finally, *control of delivery rate, rhythm* and *phrasing* will be essential to achieving clarity and effectiveness in oral communication. *Rate* may be controlled by the number and duration of the silent spaces between words and phrases, as well as by the time taken in the production of individual sounds, particularly the vowel sounds. Faster rates may be called for at times; at other times, slower rates. Variations in rate can affect the clarity of communication as well as the mood. A slow and ponderous rate may create a mood of solemnity; a rapid rate, one of lightness and joyfulness. One should vary his rate within speech to achieve variety as he varies other aspects of verbal delivery.

These variations, together with the individual's use of pauses and techniques of sound production act to generate a *rhythm of speech* that is part of the individual's style. Care should be taken that the use of pauses aids rather than hinders meaning – that pauses occur in appropriate places.

Also, special care should be taken that irrelevant sounds, such as "ah," "uh," and "um" do not creep into the individual's speech to fill up the spaces and to break up the flow of ideas. The rate and rhythm of speaking should compare favorably to a musical composition in which the breaks, accelerations, slow-downs, and repetitions add interest and clarity to the composer's purpose.

Principles Affecting Human Relations

In addition to those principles of oral communication which affect delivery, a number of principles of oral communication affect the relationship between the speaker and his audience. It should be self-evident that a listener will be more receptive to a speaker's ideas if a positive relationship exists between them. The speaker can apply certain principles which will tend to create and to maintain this type of positive relationship.

Respect the Dignity of Others

Every human being desires self-respect, a sense of personal worth, and dignity. In dealing with others it is basic to honestly nourish this desire. If we do or say anything which will injure another's dignity, if we humiliate or demean him in any way, we create resentment and antagonism which can obstruct effective communication. To implement this principle, try the following techniques in both formal and informal communications:

- *Make the other person right in something.* Even though you may disagree with him, start your search for agreement by pinpointing something in which he is right and go on from there.
- *Avoid complaining or finding fault.* The complainer and the faultfinder destroy all reasonable relations with others. Follow the maxim, "fix the error, not the blame." Protect the dignity of others by showing your respect for them personally, even while you may disagree with their ideas or criticize their work.

- *Avoid arguments.* Arguing with another implies that he is ignorant or mistaken and thereby diminishes his dignity. Antagonism can easily form around argument and obstruct effective communication. By being modest in advancing ideas and by avoiding telling others they are wrong, a speaker can reduce the possibility of damaging arguments. Rather than saying, "It is obvious that.. ..," or "Any right-thinking person can see that.. ..," try saying, "It appears to me that ....," or "Let us consider the possibility that ...."
- *Admit personal mistakes.* If one is willing to admit that he is human enough to make an error, others find their own self-image taking on increased stature.

Develop An Honest Interest in Other People

This second principle challenges us to develop an attitude of curiosity about others and to pursue this curiosity rather than to tell others about ourselves. Rather than a "Here I am" attitude, develop a "There you are" attitude. Such an attitude creates respect in others, and enables one to know those with whom he deals, to understand them, and to treat them as individuals. To cultivate an attitude of interest in others, try the following techniques:

- *Be an interested listener.* One cannot possibly respect another's point of view unless he hears it out.
- *Smile honestly and often.* A person need not agree with, approve of, or like another's point of view; understanding, recognition, and interest are sufficient to stimulate an honest smile which will reflect one's appreciation and respect for the other's point of view.
- *Ask questions frequently to understand others.* Questions are valuable because they require people to take specific actions in the direction of others. A good question reveals that one has really been listening and further, that he has an interest in what was said. And it gives another an opportunity to further reveal himself, thus providing a mechanism for getting better acquainted.

Recognize Individual Uniqueness and Worth

This third principle asks us to see people as individuals, to respond positively to their better qualities, and to understand their weaknesses. To develop ability in this area, try such methods as:

- *Get names right and use them often.* One's use of it reveals recognition of his uniqueness. Using names correctly and frequently not only satisfies the natural desire of another for recognition, but also aids a person to identify another as an individual.
- *Be appreciative and quick to give approval.* Being ready and generous with appreciation builds good human relations in two ways. It nourishes the receiver's feeling of self-esteem and worth, and it trains the giver to be observant of the strong or desirable traits and behavior of others.
- *Assume that people will behave in a good manner.* If we ascribe the best of motives and intentions to others, they will be inclined to live up to them. Assume the best of every person and you will rarely be disappointed. Assuming the best of them gives implied recognition to their worth as individuals.
- *Respect the rights and opinions of others.* A person need not always agree with the opinions of others, but he must respect the right of others to hold opinions different from his own and refrain from belittling or contradicting them.

The opinions of others are very much a part of their psychological and intellectual makeup, and to refuse respect for an opinion is to deny respect to the person himself. *Effective communication cannot occur between persons without mutual respect for their rights and opinions.*

Cooperate With the Wants of Others

This fourth principle emphasizes that behavior is directed from within a person as he attempts to satisfy his own wants or to solve his own problems. If a person seeks to communicate with others and to direct their behavior in a particular direction, he must cooperate with the wants which motivate them. That is, he must align his purposes with their wants and avoid the appearance of denying or frustrating those wants. Nevertheless, there is a difference between cooperating with the wants of others and giving in to them. Cooperation simply implies that one should present his case in a way which will reveal how the listener will benefit. Some techniques for implementing this principle follow:

- *Encourage initiative.* Great energy can be released by encouraging and tactfully guiding the initiative of others. Challenging the creative imagination of others in proposing solutions to problems; in developing plans, in organizing for action, and the like reveals the speaker's respect for the ideas of others, and can go a long way to assure their cooperation and participation in the final activity. When one's own initiative and imagination has been challenged, he is more likely to align himself with the decisions that are finally reached.
- *Help the other person get what he wants.* When another sees a person willing to help him satisfy his wants, an atmosphere conducive to effective communication and cooperation has been established. Try to recognize what others want and address the issues from their point of view.
- *Present problems and ask for solutions.* When one must ask another for help, when he must assign work, or when he wants to enlist cooperation, then he will often find it more productive to present the problem and ask for help in its solution than to make a direct demand. Instead of saying, "George, move those boxes out of the aisle," try saying, "George, these boxes are dangerous where they are; someone may injure themselves. Is there some other handy place for them where they will be out of the way?" By involving George in solving the problem you show respect for his ideas, and he will likely WANT to help solve the problem.
- *Present doubts, opinions or objections in question form.* Sometimes we must necessarily disagree with another. When it is necessary, we can make our disagreement more objective and more acceptable to others if we avoid over-positive or challenging statements. One technique for achieving this is to voice our concerns in the form of questions, which may minimize the possibility of arousing resentment or starting an argument.

Person-to-Person Communications

Not only in the public-service occupations, but also in business, industry, and everyday life, the form of communication most often used is *person-to-person speaking*. Any human activity which requires the interaction of two or more persons will rely heavily on person-to-person speaking to establish and maintain social relationships, to plan, coordinate, and carry out cooperative tasks. *Effectiveness in person-to-person communication is essential for effectiveness in most jobs.*

Informal Conversation: The major difference between conversation and public speaking is that in conversation there is give-and-take, while in public speaking the speaker does all the talking. Yet even this difference may be more apparent than actual, for in real life conversants may hold the floor for long periods of time, and public speakers may be seeking two-way communication with their audiences.

There are few firm rules of conversation that will hold true in all situations because conversational situations may vary so widely. Not only do topics vary, but the makeup of the conversants in age, occupation, interest, education may also vary. So may the time, place, and purpose of the gathering. So many situations are possible that the conversationalist who tries to meet them all in the same manner is doomed to failure. *The good conversationalist will try to develop a wise adaptability.* Some guidelines that may prove helpful are:

- Pursue only those subjects of interest to all the conversants;
- Avoid saying about another what you might resent being said about yourself;
- Avoid statements which you would be embarrassed to have repeated with your name cited as the source;
- Maintain a conversational tone: good-humored, alert, and vigorous, without being rancorous;
- Express opinions, but avoid being opinionated; contend without being contentious;
- In general, adhere to the principles of good human relations discussed in the previous section.

Interviewing: Most persons, at one time or another, have been interviewed. Public service employees, at one time or another, may be expected to conduct interviews. While interviews have many characteristics in common with conversation, there are important differences. An interview is a planned conversation – it is arranged in advance by the parties and is intended to accomplish some purpose. Interviews may be *structured* (directive) or *unstructured* (non-directive) in form. The former is likely to be task- or subject-centered and is most common in work situations. The latter are likely to be person-centered and are used for counseling, analysis, and therapy. Thus, they usually require that the interviewer have substantial professional training. There are many kinds of, and purposes for, interviews. For example:

- *Employment interviews:* for securing, developing, and training employees;
- *Induction interviews:* for orienting new employees;
- *Performance review interviews:* for training, and developing employees;
- *Counseling interviews:* for personal and personnel matters;
- *Correction interviews:* for disciplining and guidance of staff;
- *Grievance interviews:* reverse correction interviews;
- *Data gathering interviews:* to obtain special information;
- *Consulting interviews:* exchange of information and problem-solving with an expert;
- *Sales interviews:* for persuading another;
- *Order-giving interviews:* to assign tasks and procedures;
- *Exit interviews:* a debriefing of an employee upon separation.

From the above it can be seen that interviews are directed toward serving three basic goals:

- to increase understanding through information-giving and information-getting;

- to persuade; and
- to solve problems.

To be effective, interviews should be carefully planned. Objectives should be determined in advance, and thought should be given to major obstacles likely to arise. The strategy and tactics of the interview should be planned beforehand, and consideration should be given to some contingency plans in the event that certain events occur during the interview.

The beginning of the interview should establish a workable arrangement between the parties by establishing an appropriate atmosphere, stimulating interest and attention, and presenting the problem or goal of the interview. The body of the interview should pursue the above objectives.

The close of the interview should round out and gracefully terminate the interview. The gist of the interview should be reviewed or summarized; the bases for further conversations should be established if necessary; and appreciations should be expressed.

Group Discussions: The term "group discussion" describes an activity that enables a number of cooperative people to talk freely about a problem under the leadership of a member of the group. They have the common purpose of interchanging ideas for specific needs. Group discussion is sometimes confused with debate, but the two activities differ in purpose, in format, and in the attitude of the participants. *The purpose of debate is advocacy; the purpose of discussion is inquiry.*

In group discussion, the participants deliberate seriously with minimum restraints. They work in cooperation with one another in discussion at least until the group as a unit has reached a solution to a problem. Their purpose is to inquire in order to learn all aspects of a problem, and then to solve it. Although participants may disagree, their purpose is to sort out the areas of agreement in arriving at answers.

Techniques of Group Discussion: The techniques and formats of group discussion may vary, but the underlying purpose remains the same – to inquire into the essential aspects of a problem and to solve it. Some types of discussions, such as the *meeting,* or *round-table,* are not intended for audiences; others, such as the *panel,* the *symposium,* and the *forum,* are planned for audiences. Whatever the format, the participants should remember that they are acting as a group studying a question. It requires real skill on the part of all participants to pool relevant information, to move the discussion forward, to limit heated cross talk, and to stress areas of agreements.

Criteria for group discussion: Group discussion is useful only if the group has a real problem to solve and if its members all agree on what that is. Thus, stating the question in an effective way is important to promote fruitful discussion. Here are some criteria for worthwhile discussions:
- The problem should deserve a solution.
- The problem should be worth the time spent on it.
- The problem should be either timely or timeless.
- The problem should be able to be solved in the time available.
- The group should be competent to solve the problem.
- The problem should be stated in question form.

- The question for discussion should not be stated in a form demanding a "yes" or "no" answer, but in a form indicating a need for discussion. (Instead of: "Should the federal government control the press?" try: "What should be the role of the federal government in regulating the press?")

Leading a discussion requires some special skills. The discussion leader must insure the orderly, systematic, and cooperative consideration of the question. He tries to direct the course of the discussion without manipulating the group to accept any particular conclusion. He assures that every member of the group has an opportunity to participate, and that no one monopolizes the floor. He provides needed facts or calls upon others to provide them. He summarizes when needed and restates the issues under discussion. He strives to keep the emphasis upon agreement and cooperative thinking in order to avoid conflict.

A simple functional plan for discussion leadership might include the following steps for a problem-solving discussion:
- Introduction of the problem by the leader
- Defining potentially confusing terms
- Presentation of relevant facts by group members
- Specifying criteria for judging a good solution
- Presentation by members of possible solutions
- Analysis of solutions in relation to criteria
- Decision: which solution is preferred, or what additional information is needed before a decision can be made

Forms of group discussion: Several forms of group discussion are in common use. Each occasion for group discussion implies its own format for discussion that will best serve its own specific needs, purposes, and interests. The common formats include:
- The *round table* (or informal) group discussion is usually not observed by an audience. The preferred number of participants is from four to seven, although good discussions may be held with as many as fifteen or as few as three participants. The discussants should cooperate courteously in reaching a decision. Formal recognition to speak is not necessary. The outstanding characteristic of the round-table discussion is its informality.
- The *panel* is similar except for the presence of an audience. With an audience, the members are more formal in their presentations, speaking not only for themselves, but for the audience as well. If the audience participates by asking questions after the solution has been reached, the activity is called a *panel forum.*
- A *symposium* differs from the panel or round-table because all participants, perhaps three or four, are experts on phases of the question. The speakers give set speeches in order and are provided little opportunity for interchanging ideas with their fellow participants. The symposium is typically presented for the benefit of an audience. Often a panel follows a symposium, offering the participants an opportunity, after their individual presentations, to exchange ideas in a discussion format. When the audience is invited to ask questions of the participants, the activity is called a *symposium-forum.*
- The *forum* is an activity distinguished by audience participation. The forum may be used in combination with a panel, a symposium, a lecture, a debate, or any other form that may be useful to communicate basic information to the

audience prior to its participation. The leader, in conducting a forum, should explain the procedures to be followed by members of the audience in asking questions or making comments, including how to be recognized, how much time will be allowed, and the like.

Group discussion is an excellent means of pooling knowledge, reaching decisions, and informing the public. The public-service employee will find himself participating in group discussion both within his organization, at staff meetings and other groups, and for audiences as a means of informing public opinion.

Speaking Before Groups

The distinction between speaking IN a group and speaking BEFORE a group is not always apparent. If, as a member of a group, one speaks his piece for five full minutes without interruption, or if he rises and speaks from a standing position, is he speaking in the group or before it? While it is a popular notion that group speaking, or public speaking is characterized by a much higher degree of formality, and by one-way communication from the speaker to his audience, it is well to consider speaking before a group as simply dignified, amplified conversation. *Public speaking, at its best, seeks to establish a carefully planned conversational relationship with a group of persons.*

The public-service employee will find many occasions in which he will be called upon to speak before a group. The group may be his co-workers, as at a staff or committee meeting; his colleagues, as at a professional conference; or members of the public, as at a public meeting, or a meeting of a citizens' group. Whatever the particular occasion, the employee may be called upon to speak before a group for any of several purposes. The general principles of effective oral communication apply to public or group speaking, as well as to person-to-person speaking, and attention to these principles will aid in developing effectiveness in speaking before groups. Public-service employees commonly participate in speaking before groups for the purposes of informing, instructing, persuading, motivating, or entertaining.

Speaking to Inform

The primary purpose of the speech to inform is to convey information to listeners to clarify a point of view, a process, a method, an idea, a problem, or a proposed solution. By far the greatest amount of speaking before a group is done to convey information. The content may vary from relatively simple, concrete topics, such as how to complete a personnel form, to highly abstract topics, such as how a client-centered program will affect relations with clients.

Three general types of informing speeches are commonly used in public-service work:

- reports
- briefings
- informational talks

An *oral report* summarizes in orderly fashion a body of information, usually assembled by the person making the report.

A *briefing* is similar to a report, except that it usually occurs as a prelude to some imminent action. All the facts needed for decision-making actions are assembled immediately before the action, and conveyed to those who will be making the decisions.

The *informational talk* is less formal, usually delivered by a knowledgeable person without need for much formal preparation. An informational talk might be presented by the head of an agency about the agency's work to a group of new employees. A simple and typical four-part outline for information speeches consists of the following parts:

- Introduction – tell them what you are going to tell them
- Key Idea – tell them the main or central idea
- Body – tell them the details
- Conclusion – tell them what you told them

Speaking to Instruct

Almost every employee in a public agency at one time or another will be expected to teach or train others. This teaching will often occur in a group situation, and the employee will function as a teacher, speaking to the group, assigning practice, evaluating student work, and similar activities. Speaking for this purpose should generally follow the rules of good human relations, of course, but additionally should use certain principles of learning which will increase the effectiveness of teaching.

When speaking to instruct or train a group, the instructor should employ the following principles:

- *Include an advance organizer:* A summary of the tasks that will be learned, and a reason for learning them
- *Provide active practice:* Give the learners, or listeners, plenty of opportunity to practice what you want them to learn. Ask a lot of questions; hand out worksheets; break the group into "buzz" groups for discussion; get them actively involved.
- *Help them succeed:* Don't assign them work or ask them questions which they are likely to fail. Give them hints if necessary during practice, but help them succeed.
- *Give them plenty of feedback:* If they answer a question correctly, or turn in a correct worksheet, or make a correct contribution in some other way, let them know it right away. Not tomorrow, or next week, but let them know immediately.

If these principles can be incorporated into instructional talks and training sessions, they are likely to be more effective.

Speaking to Persuade

The public-service employee may find himself speaking to persuade a group from time to time. In ordinary work situations, he may wish to persuade his fellow workers to adopt a new policy, or a certain attitude toward their work. On other occasions, he may be speaking to members of the public, trying to persuade them favorably toward his agency, or to avail themselves of the agency's program.

Basically, there are three types of appeals that the speaker can make to his audience:

- *Logical Appeals:* Through the use of deductive reasoning (from general ideas to specific conclusion) and inductive reasoning (from specific data to a general conclusion), and the presenting of factual evidence to support this reasoning, the speaker appeals mainly to the listener's intellect and reason.

- *Psychological Appeals:* Through appeals to the listener's motivations, feelings and values, the speaker tries to get his listeners to WANT to adopt the idea being presented.
- *Personal Appeals:* Through his own personal effect, the speaker tries to influence his listeners – by characterizing his own reputation, appearance, personality and character in a way that will create a favorable and receptive climate for his ideas.

Beyond these types of appeals, the persuasive speaker will do well to attend carefully to the principles of good human relations discussed earlier.

Speaking to Motivate

Another occasion for speaking before a group is to motivate them – to excite, arouse, or spur them on. Usually such speaking is occasioned by some strong feelings in the speaker about his subject. He may, for example, feel that the staff of the agency is simply not attaching sufficient importance to certain areas of their work. At a staff meeting he might address the group and try to get them "fired up" about that work.

Speaking of this type generally follows the patterns of the persuasive speech, since we often are seeking to influence the listeners in a particular direction. Typically, however, its appeal tends to focus upon the psychological, since the speaker is usually more interested in affecting attitudes, motivations, and values than he is in affecting beliefs.

Speaking to Entertain

While not normally central to the duties of public-service employees, the entertaining speech is an occasional responsibility that may fall to almost anyone. At an annual dinner, a staff party, an agency picnic, one may be called upon to speak briefly to a group in a light and casual tone. When called upon on such an occasion, one should be especially aware that he need not be uproariously funny to be entertaining. *To entertain means simply to amuse or to divert.*

It is well to recognize that few persons have the practiced skills of a professional comedian to keep an audience laughing from start to finish. The occasional speaker who seeks to entertain an audience, to amuse and divert them for a few brief moments, does well to adapt his humor to the local and familiar experiences of his audience.
In general, the entertaining speech should attend to the principles of good human relations. The speaker should not develop humor at the expense of any person's dignity. While he may poke gentle fun at himself, rarely can one poke fun at others without injuring their dignity and self-esteem. As with other purposeful speeches, speeches to entertain may be organized around the four-part outline discussed earlier.

STUDENT LEARNING ACTIVITIES
- Prepare a list of principles affecting delivery, and a list of principles affecting human relations. Develop checklists for evaluating the speech of others based upon these principles.
- Participate in informal conversation with two others before the class. No topic should be decided in advance. Following the conversation, participate in a class critique of the conversation.
- Participate in two interview situations set up by your teacher. In one, function as the interviewer; in the other, as the interviewee.

- Participate in a round-table discussion on a problem assigned by your teacher.
- Participate in a panel-forum on a problem assigned by your teacher.
- Participate as a member of a symposium-forum on a problem assigned by your teacher.
- Prepare and present a 5-minute oral report on a topic assigned by your teacher.
- Prepare and present a 5-minute lesson on a subject assigned by your teacher.
- Prepare and present a 5-minute persuasive or motivational speech on a subject assigned by your teacher.
- Prepare and present a 5-minute speech to entertain the class.
- Participate in critiques of the speeches and discussions involving other students. Use principles of delivery and human relations as the basis for your criticism.

TEACHER MANAGEMENT ACTIVITIES

- Have each student develop checklists for critiquing oral communications based upon the principles of delivery and human relations discussed in the first topic. Through class discussion, develop a checklist evaluation form that will be used by the class for evaluating speech performance.
- Have students in groups of three participate in informal conversations. Topics should not be decided in advance. The setting should be informal as possible. But the conversation should be observed and evaluated by members of the class. "Buzz" groups may be formed, with teams of "evaluators" dropping into the groups.
- Assign interview situations to pairs of students, designating the interviews and the interviewees. Students should be given ten or fifteen minutes to prepare for their part of the interview. Interviews should be critiqued by the class.
- Assign students to round-table panel and symposium groups. Assign each a problem to discuss. Have each group discuss its problem before the class. Critique the discussions.
- Have each student prepare a five-minute report, a five-minute lesson on some subject, a five-minute persuasive speech, a five-minute entertainment speech, on topics you approve. Presentations should be evaluated by the class using the critique forms developed by the class.

EVALUATION QUESTIONS

1. Effective speakers have voices that: 1._____
   A. Have a pleasant pitch and volume
   B. Lack variety of pitch
   C. Have great volume
   D. Have a very high pitch

2. A competent speaker would: 2._____
   A. Look at the people in the front row
   B. Look at the people in the back row
   C. Look at all the people in the group
   D. Look at the people in the middle of the group

3. Looking at the audience is helpful to the speaker because: 3._____
     A. It helps the speaker watch for audience reaction
     B. It helps the speaker watch for signs of misunderstanding
     C. It enables the speaker to pick out signs of doubt
     D. All of the above

4. An effective speaker would: 4._____
     A. Look lively and sincere
     B. Keep his face as blank as possible
     C. Look overly composed;
     D. Look disinterested about the subject

5. Body language can indicate: 5._____
     A. Emphasis
     B. Firmness of purpose
     C. Indifference
     D. All of the above

6. These items would be included in a group of visual aids: 6._____
     A. Phonograph records and record player
     B. Charts, graphs, and maps
     C. Tape decks and cassettes
     D. All of the above

7. It is preferable for a speaker to use: 7._____
     A. Many abstract and general words
     B. Precise words
     C. Fancy words
     D. Round-about expressions

8. As a speaker, you should: 8._____
     A. Use your own language
     B. Pattern your language after someone else
     C. Imitate highly educated people
     D. Use the occasion to try out big words you are learning

9. Accomplished speakers: 9._____
     A. Deliver their speeches as fast as they can to economize time
     B. Deliver their speeches at a very slow rate
     C. Give very solemn speeches at a rapid rate
     D. Vary the rate within the speech to achieve variety

10. An effective speaker would: 10._____
     A. Speak rapidly without leaving any break between sentences
     B. Fill up the spaces by saying "ah"
     C. Pause occasionally
     D. Use "you know" to fill in

11. A good technique in human relations is to: 11._____
  A. Tell others they are wrong about everything
  B. Point out the other person's faults
  C. Admit your own mistakes
  D. Attack others personally

12. The most sought after people are those who: 12._____
  A. Tell others all about themselves
  B. Are good listeners
  C. Smile only when necessary
  D. Let others know how they feel about every subject

13. For a person who has recently been hired, it is preferable to: 13._____
  A. Be quick to show what others are doing wrong
  B. Be suspicious of others until they prove themselves
  C. Try to convince others to think as you do on every subject
  D. None of the above

14. A good technique in human relations is to: 14._____
  A. Ask the opinions of others
  B. Help other people get what they want
  C. Present your doubts in the form of a question
  D. All of the above

Answer Key

1. A	4. A	7. B	10. C	13. D
2. C	5. D	8. A	11. C	14. D
3. D	6. B	9. D	12. B	

PRINCIPLES AND PRACTICES OF ADMINISTRATION, SUPERVISION & MANAGEMENT

TABLE OF CONTENTS

PRINCIPLES AND PRACTICES OF
ADMINISTRATION, SUPERVISION & MANAGEMENT

Most people are inclined to think of administration as something that only a few persons are responsible for in a large organization. Perhaps this is true if you are thinking of Administration with a capital *A*, but administration with a lower case a is a responsibility of supervisors at all levels each working day.

All of us feel we are pretty good supervisors and that we do a good job of administering the workings of our agency. By and large, this is true, but every so often it is good to check up on ourselves. Checklists appear from time to time in various publications which psychologists say, tell whether or not a person will make a good wife, husband, doctor, lawyer, or supervisor.

The following questions are an excellent checklist to test yourself as a supervisor and administrator.

Remember, Administration gives direction and points the way but administration carries the ideas to fruition. Each is dependent on the other for its success. Remember, too, that no unit is too small for these departmental functions to be carried out. These statements apply equally as well to the Chief Librarian as to the Department Head with but one or two persons to supervise.

GENERAL ADMINISTRATION - General Responsibilities of Supervisors

1.   Have I prepared written statements of functions, activities, and duties for my organizational unit?

2.   Have I prepared procedural guides for operating activities?

3.   Have I established clearly in writing, lines of authority and responsibility for my organizational unit?

4.   Do I make recommendations for improvements in organization, policies, administrative and operating routines and procedures, including simplification of work and elimination of non-essential operations?

5.   Have I designated and trained an understudy to function in my absence?

6.   Do I supervise and train personnel within the unit to effectively perform their assignments?

7.   Do I assign personnel and distribute work on such a basis as to carry out the organizational unit's assignment or mission in the most effective and efficient manner?

8.   Have I established administrative controls by:

    a.   Fixing responsibility and accountability on all supervisors under my direction for the proper performance of their functions and duties.

b.   Preparing and submitting periodic work load and progress reports covering the operations of the unit to my immediate superior.

c.   Analysis and evaluation of such reports received from subordinate units.

d.   Submission of significant developments and problems arising within the organizational unit to my immediate superior.

e.   Conducting conferences, inspections, etc., as to the status and efficiency of unit operations.

9.   Do I maintain an adequate and competent working force?

10.   Have I fostered good employee-department relations, seeing that established rules, regulations, and instructions are being carried out properly?

11.   Do I collaborate and consult with other organizational units performing related functions to insure harmonious and efficient working relationships?

12.   Do I maintain liaison through prescribed channels with city departments and other governmental agencies concerned with the activities of the unit?

13.   Do I maintain contact with and keep abreast of the latest developments and techniques of administration (professional societies, groups, periodicals, etc.) as to their applicability to the activities of the unit?

14.   Do I communicate with superiors and subordinates through prescribed organizational channels?

15.   Do I notify superiors and subordinates in instances where bypassing is necessary as soon thereafter as practicable?

16.   Do I keep my superior informed of significant developments and problems?

SEVEN BASIC FUNCTIONS OF THE SUPERVISOR

1.   PLANNING
This means working out goals and means to obtain goals. <u>What</u> needs to be done, <u>who</u> will do it, <u>how</u>, <u>when</u>, and <u>where</u> it is to be done.

SEVEN STEPS IN PLANNING

1.   Define job or problem clearly.
2.   Consider priority of job.
3.   Consider time-limit - starting and completing.
4.   Consider minimum distraction to, or interference with, other activities.
5.   Consider and provide for contingencies - possible emergencies.
6.   Break job down into components.
7.   Consider the 5 W's and H:

WHY	...	is it necessary to do the job? (Is the purpose clearly defined?)
WHAT	...	needs to be done to accomplish the defined purpose?
	...	is needed to do the job? (money, materials, etc.)
WHO	...	is needed to do the job?
	...	will have responsibilities?
WHERE	...	is the work to be done?
WHEN	...	is the job to begin and end? (schedules, etc.)
HOW	...	is the job to be done? (methods, controls, records, etc.)

2. ORGANIZING

This means dividing up the work, establishing clear lines of responsibility and authority and coordinating efforts to get the job done.

3. STAFFING

The whole personnel function of bringing in and training staff, getting the right man and fitting him to the right job - the job to which he is best suited.

In the normal situation, the supervisor's responsibility regarding staffing normally includes providing accurate job descriptions, that is, duties of the jobs, requirements, education and experience, skills, physical, etc.; assigning the work for maximum use of skills; and proper utilization of the probationary period to weed out unsatisfactory employees.

4. DIRECTING

Providing the necessary leadership to the group supervised. Important work gets done to the supervisor's satisfaction.

5. COORDINATING

The all-important duty of inter-relating the various parts of the work.

The supervisor is also responsible for controlling the coordinated activities. This means measuring performance according to a time schedule and setting quotas to see that the goals previously set are being reached. Reports from workers should be analyzed, evaluated, and made part of all future plans.

6. REPORTING

This means proper and effective communication to your superiors, subordinates, and your peers (in definition of the job of the supervisor). Reports should be read and information contained therein should be used not be filed away and forgotten. Reports should be written in such a way that the desired action recommended by the report is forthcoming.

7. BUDGETING

This means controlling current costs and forecasting future costs. This forecast is based on past experience, future plans and programs, as well as current costs.

You will note that these seven functions can fall under three topics:

Planning	)	
Organizing	)	Make a Plan
Staffing	)	
Directing	)	Get things done
Controlling	)	

Reporting   )
Budgeting   )   Watch it work

PLANNING TO MEET MANAGEMENT GOALS

I. <u>WHAT IS PLANNING?</u>
    A. Thinking a job through before new work is done to determine the best way to do it
    B. A method of doing something
    C. Ways and means for achieving set goals
    D. A means of enabling a supervisor to deliver with a minimum of effort, all details involved in coordinating his work

II. <u>WHO SHOULD MAKE PLANS?</u>
Everybody!
All levels of supervision must plan work. (Top management, heads of divisions or bureaus, first line supervisors, and individual employees.) The higher the level, the more planning required.

III. <u>WHAT ARE THE RESULTS OF POOR PLANNING?</u>
    A. Failure to meet deadline
    B. Low employee morale
    C. Lack of job coordination
    D. Overtime is frequently necessary
    E. Excessive cost, waste of material and manhours

IV. <u>PRINCIPLES OF PLANNING</u>
    A. Getting a clear picture of your objectives. What exactly are you trying to accomplish?
    B. Plan the whole job, then the parts, in proper sequence.
    C. Delegate the planning of details to those responsible for executing them.
    D. Make your plan flexible.
    E. Coordinate your plan with the plans of others so that the work may be processed with a minimum of delay.
    F. Sell your plan before you execute it.
    G. Sell your plan to your superior, subordinate, in order to gain maximum participation and coordination.
    H. Your plan should take precedence. Use knowledge and skills that others have brought to a similar job.
    I. Your plan should take account of future contingencies; allow for future expansion.
    J. Plans should include minor details. Leave nothing to chance that can be anticipated.
    K. Your plan should be simple and provide standards and controls. Establish quality and quantity standards and set a standard method of doing the job. The controls will indicate whether the job is proceeding according to plan.
    L. Consider possible bottlenecks, breakdowns, or other difficulties that are likely to arise.

V. Q. WHAT ARE THE *YARDSTICKS* BY WHICH PLANNING SHOULD BE MEASURED?
    A. Any plan should:
      - Clearly state a definite course of action to be followed and goal to be achieved, with consideration for emergencies.
      - Be realistic and practical.

- State what's to be done, when it's to be done, where, how, and by whom.
- Establish the most efficient sequence of operating steps so that more is accomplished in less time, with the least effort, and with the best quality results.
- Assure meeting deliveries without delays.
- Establish the standard by which performance is to be judged.

Q. WHAT KINDS OF PLANS DOES EFFECTIVE SUPERVISION REQUIRE?
A. Plans should cover such factors as:
- Manpower - right number of properly trained employees on the job.
- Materials - adequate supply of the right materials and supplies.
- Machines - full utilization of machines and equipment, with proper maintenance.
- Methods - most efficient handling of operations.
- Deliveries - making deliveries on time.
- Tools - sufficient well-conditioned tools
- Layout - most effective use of space.
- Reports - maintaining proper records and reports.
- Supervision - planning work for employees and organizing supervisor's own time.

I. <u>MANAGEMENT</u>

Question: *What do we mean by management?*

Answer: *Getting work done through others.*

Management could also be defined as planning, directing, and controlling the operations of a bureau or division so that all factors will function properly and all persons cooperate efficiently for a common objective.

II. <u>MANAGEMENT PRINCIPLES</u>

1. There should be a hierarchy - wherein authority and responsibility run upward and downward through several levels - with a broad base at the bottom and a single head at the top.

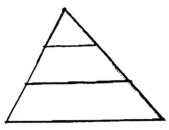

2. Each and every unit or person in the organization should be answerable ultimately to the manager at the apex. In other words, *The buck stops here!*

3. Every necessary function involved in the bureau's objectives is assigned to a unit in that bureau.

4. Responsibilities assigned to a unit are specifically clear-cut and understood.

5. Consistent methods of organizational structure should be applied at each level of the organization.

6. Each member of the bureau from top to bottom knows:
to whom he reports
who reports to him.

7. No member of one bureau reports to more than one supervisor.
No dual functions

8. Responsibility for a function is matched by authority necessary to perform that function.
Weight of authority

9. Individuals or units reporting to a supervisor do not exceed the number which can be feasibly and effectively coordinated and directed.
Concept of *span of control*

10. Channels of command (management) are not violated by staff units, although there should be staff services to facilitate and coordinate management functions.

11. Authority and responsibility should be decentralized to units and individuals who are responsible for the actual performance of operations.
Welfare - down to Welfare Centers
Hospitals - down to local hospitals

12. Management should exercise control through attention to policy problems of exceptional importance, rather than through review of routine actions of subordinates.

13. Organizations should never be permitted to grow so elaborate as to hinder work accomplishments.
Empire building

II. ORGANIZATION STRUCTURE
Types of Organizations.
The purest form is a leader and a few followers, such as:

```
                    | Supervisor |
  | Worker |   | Worker |   | Worker |   | Worker |
```

(Refer to organization chart) from supervisor to workers.

The line of authority is direct, The workers know exactly where they stand in relation to their boss, to whom they report for instructions and direction.

Unfortunately, in our present complex society, few organizations are similar to this example of a pure line organization. In this era of specialization, other people are often needed in the simplest of organizations. These specialists are known as staff. The sole purpose for their existence (staff) is to assist, advise, suggest, help or counsel line organizations. Staff has no authority to direct line people - nor do they give them direct instructions.

```
                    ┌─────────────┐
                    │ SUPERVISOR  │
                    └─────────────┘
                           │
   ┌───────────────┬───────┴───────┬───────────────┐
┌──────────┐  ┌──────────┐   ┌──────────┐   ┌────────┐
│ Personnel│  │Accounting│   │Inspection│   │ Legal  │
└──────────┘  └──────────┘   └──────────┘   └────────┘
 ┌────────┐    ┌────────┐     ┌────────┐     ┌────────┐
 │ Worker │    │ Worker │     │ Worker │     │ Worker │
 └────────┘    └────────┘     └────────┘     └────────┘
```

Line Functions	Staff Functions
1. Directs	1. Advises
2. Orders	2. Persuades and sells
3. Responsibility for carrying out activities from beginning to end	3. Staff studies, reports, recommends but does not carry out
4. Follows chain of command	4. May advise across department lines
5. Is identified with what it does	5. May find its ideas identified with others
6. Decides when and how to use staff advice	6. Has to persuade line to want its advice
7. Line executes	7. Staff - Conducts studies and research. Provides advice and instructions in technical matters. Serves as technical specialist to render specific services

Types and Functions of Organization Charts.
An organization chart is a picture of the arrangement and inter-relationship of the subdivisions of an organization.

1. Types of Charts:
   a. Structural - basic relationships only
   b. Functional - includes functions or duties
   c. Personnel - positions, salaries, status, etc.
   d. Process Chart - work performed
   e. Gantt Chart - actual performance against planned
   f. Flow Chart - flow and distribution of work

2. Functions of Charts:
   a. Assist in management planning and control
   b. Indicate duplication of functions
   c. Indicate incorrect stressing of functions
   d. Indicate neglect of important functions
   e. Correct unclear authority
   f. Establish proper span of control

3. Limitations of Charts:
   a. Seldom maintained on current basis

    b.   Chart is oversimplified

    c.   Human factors cannot adequately be charted

4. Organization Charts should be:

    a.   Simple

    b.   Symmetrical

    c.   Indicate authority

    d.   Line and staff relationship differentiated

    e.   Chart should be dated and bear signature of approving officer

    f.   Chart should be displayed, not hidden

ORGANIZATION

There are four basic principles of organization:

1.   Unity of command
2.   Span of control
3.   Uniformity of assignment
4.   Assignment of responsibility and delegation of authority

Unity of Command

Unity of command means that each person in the organization should receive orders from one, and only one, supervisor. When a person has to take orders from two or more people, (a) the orders may be in conflict and the employee is upset because he does not know which he should obey, or, (b) different orders may reach him at the same time and he does not know which he should carry out first.

Equally as bad as having two bosses is the situation where the supervisor is by-passed. Let us suppose you are a supervisor whose boss by-passes you (deals directly with people reporting to you). To the worker, it is the same as having two bosses; but to you, the supervisor, it is equally serious. By-passing on the part of your boss will undermine your authority, and the people under you will begin looking to your boss for decisions and even for routine orders.

You can prevent by-passing by telling the people you supervise that if anyone tries to give them orders, they should direct that person to you.

Span of Control

Span of control on a given level involves:

    a.   The number of people being supervised

    b.   The distance

    c.   The time involved in supervising the people. (One supervisor cannot supervise too many workers effectively.)

Span of control means that a supervisor has the right number (not too many and not too few) of subordinates that he can supervise well.

Uniformity of Assignment

In assigning work, you as the supervisor should assign to each person jobs that are similar in nature. An employee who is assigned too many different types of jobs will waste time in going from one kind of work to another. It takes time for him to get to top production in one kind of task and, before he does so, he has to start on another.

When you assign work to people, remember that:

a.   Job duties should be definite. Make it clear from the beginning <u>what</u> they are to do, <u>how</u> they are to do it, and <u>why</u> they are to do it. Let them know how much they are expected to do and how well they are expected to do it.

b.   Check your assignments to be certain that there are no workers with too many unrelated duties, and that no two people have been given overlapping responsibilities. Your aim should be to have every task assigned to a specific person with the work fairly distributed and with each person doing his part.

<u>Assignment of Responsibility and Delegation of Authority</u>

A supervisor cannot delegate his final responsibility for the work of his department. The experienced supervisor knows that he gets his work done through people. He can't do it all himself. So he must assign the work and the responsibility for the work to his employees. Then they must be given the authority to carry out their responsibilities.

By assigning responsibility and delegating authority to carry out the responsibility, the supervisor builds in his workers initiative, resourcefulness, enthusiasm, and interest in their work. He is treating them as responsible adults. They can find satisfaction in their work, and they will respect the supervisor and be loyal to the supervisor.

PRINCIPLES OF ORGANIZATION

1.   <u>Definition</u>
Organization is the method of dividing up the work to provide the best channels for coordinated effort to get the agency's mission accomplished.

2.   <u>Purpose of Organization</u>
a.   To enable each employee within the organization to clearly know his responsibilities and relationships to his fellow employees and to organizational units.
b.   To avoid conflicts of authority and overlapping of jurisdiction.
c.   To ensure teamwork.

3.   <u>Basic Considerations in Organizational Planning</u>
a.   The basic plans and objectives of the agency should be determined, and the organizational structure should be adapted to carry out effectively such plans and objectives.
b.   The organization should be built around the major functions of the agency and not individuals or groups of individuals.
c.   The organization should be sufficiently flexible to meet new and changing conditions which may be brought about from within or outside the department.
d.   The organizational structure should be as simple as possible and the number of organizational units kept at a minimum.
e.   The number of levels of authority should be kept at a minimum. Each additional management level lengthens the chain of authority and responsibility and increases the time for instructions to be distributed to operating levels and for decisions to be obtained from higher authority.

    f.   The form of organization should permit each executive to exercise maximum initiative within the limits of delegated authority.

4.   Bases for Organization
    a.   Purpose (Examples: education, police, sanitation)
    b.   Process (Examples: accounting, legal, purchasing)
    c.   Clientele (Examples: welfare, parks, veteran)
    d.   Geographic (Examples: borough offices, precincts, libraries)

5.   Assignments of Functions
    a.   Every function of the agency should be assigned to a specific organizational unit. Under normal circumstances, no single function should be assigned to more than one organizational unit.
    b.   There should be no overlapping, duplication, or conflict between organizational elements.
    c.   Line functions should be separated from staff functions, and proper emphasis should be placed on staff activities.
    d.   Functions which are closely related or similar should normally be assigned to a single organizational unit.
    e.   Functions should be properly distributed to promote balance, and to avoid overemphasis of less important functions and underemphasis of more essential functions.

6.   Delegation of Authority and Responsibility
    a.   Responsibilities assigned to a specific individual or organizational unit should carry corresponding authority, and all statements of authority or limitations thereof should be as specific as possible.
    b.   Authority and responsibility for action should be decentralized to organizational units and individuals responsible for actual performance to the greatest extent possible, without relaxing necessary control over policy or the standardization of procedures. Delegation of authority will be consistent with decentralization of responsibility but such delegation will not divest an executive in higher authority of his overall responsibility.
    c.   The heads of organizational units should concern themselves with important matters and should delegate to the maximum extent details and routines performed in the ordinary course of business.
    d.   All responsibilities, authorities, and relationships should be stated in simple language to avoid misinterpretation.
    e.   Each individual or organizational unit charged with a specific responsibility will be held responsible for results.

7.   Employee Relationships
    a.   The employees reporting to one executive should not exceed the number which can be effectively directed and coordinated. The number will depend largely upon the scope and extent of the responsibilities of the subordinates.
    b.   No person should report to more than one supervisor. Every supervisor should know who reports to him, and every employee should know to whom he reports. Channels of authority and responsibility should not be violated by staff units.
    c.   Relationships between organizational units within the agency and with outside organizations and associations should be clearly stated and thoroughly understood to avoid misunderstanding.

DELEGATING

1. <u>What is Delegating?</u>
Delegating is assigning a job to an employee, giving him the authority to get that job done, and giving him the responsibility for seeing to it that the job is done.

   a. <u>What to Delegate</u>
   (1) Routine details
   (2) Jobs which may be necessary and take a lot of time, but do not have to be done by the supervisor personally (preparing reports, attending meetings, etc.)
   (3) Routine decision-making (making decisions which do not require the supervisor's personal attention)

   b. <u>What Not to Delegate</u>
   (1) Job details which are *executive functions* (setting goals, organizing employees into a good team, analyzing results so as to plan for the future)
   (2) Disciplinary power (handling grievances, preparing service ratings, reprimands, etc.)
   (3) Decision-making which involves large numbers of employees or other bureaus and departments
   (4) Final and complete responsibility for the job done by the unit being supervised

   c. <u>Why Delegate?</u>
   (1) To strengthen the organization by developing a greater number of skilled employees
   (2) To improve the employee's performance by giving him the chance to learn more about the job, handle some responsibility, and become more interested in getting the job done
   (3) To improve a supervisor's performance by relieving him of routine jobs and giving him more time for *executive functions* (planning, organizing, controlling, etc.) which cannot be delegated

2. <u>To Whom to Delegate</u>
People with abilities not being used. Selection should be based on ability, not on favoritism.

REPORTS

<u>Definition</u>
A report is an orderly presentation of factual information directed to a specific reader for a specific purpose.

<u>Purpose</u>
The general purpose of a report is to bring to the reader useful and factual information about a condition or a problem. Some specific purposes of a report may be:

1. To enable the reader to appraise the efficiency or effectiveness of a person or an operation
2. To provide a basis for establishing standards
3. To reflect the results of expenditures of time, effort, and money
4. To provide a basis for developing or altering programs

Types

1. Information Report - Contains facts arranged in sequence
2. Summary (Examination) Report - Contains facts plus an analysis or discussion of the significance of the facts. Analysis may give advantages and disadvantages or give qualitative and quantitative comparisons
3. Recommendation Report - Contains facts, analysis, and conclusion logically drawn from the facts and analysis, plus a recommendation based upon the facts, analysis, and conclusions

Factors to Consider Before Writing Report

1. <u>Why</u> write the report - The purpose of the report should be clearly defined.
2. <u>Who</u> will read the report - What level of language should be used? Will the reader understand professional or technical language?
3. <u>What</u> should be said - What does the reader need or want to know about the subject?
4. <u>How</u> should it be said - Should the subject be presented tactfully? Convincingly? In a stimulating manner?

Preparatory Steps

1. Assemble the facts - Find out who, why, what, where, when, and how.
2. Organize the facts - Eliminate unnecessary information.
3. Prepare an outline - Check for orderliness, logical sequence.
4. Prepare a draft - Check for correctness, clearness, completeness, conciseness, and tone.
5. Prepare it in final form - Check for grammar, punctuation, appearance.

Outline For a Recommendation Report
Is the report:

1. Correct in information, grammar, and tone?
2. Clear?
3. Complete?
4. Concise?
5. Timely?
6. Worth its cost?

Will the report accomplish its purpose?

MANAGEMENT CONTROLS

1. <u>Control</u>
What is control? What is controlled? Who controls?

The essence of control is action which adjusts operations to predetermined standards, and its basis is information in the hands of managers. Control is checking to determine whether plans are being observed and suitable progress toward stated objectives is being made, and action is taken, if necessary, to correct deviations.

We have a ready-made model for this concept of control in the automatic systems which are widely used for process control in the chemical and petroleum industries. A process control system works this way. Suppose, for example, it is desired to maintain a constant rate of flow of oil through a pipe at a predetermined or set-point value. A signal, whose strength represents the rate of flow, can be produced in a measuring device and transmitted to a control mechanism. The control mechanism, when it detects any deviation of the actual from the set-point signal, will reposition the value regulating flow rate.

2. Basis For Control

    A process control mechanism thus acts to adjust operations to predetermined standards and does so on the basis of information it receives. In a parallel way, information reaching a manager gives him the opportunity for corrective action and is his basis for control. He cannot exercise control without such information, and he cannot do a complete job of managing without controlling.

3. Policy
    What is policy?

    Policy is simply a statement of an organization's intention to act in certain ways when specified types of circumstances arise. It represents a general decision, predetermined and expressed as a principle or rule, establishing a normal pattern of conduct for dealing with given types of business events - usually recurrent. A statement is therefore useful in economizing the time of managers and in assisting them to discharge their responsibilities equitably and consistently.

    Policy is not a means of control, but policy does generate the need for control.

    Adherence to policies is not guaranteed nor can it be taken on faith. It has to be verified. Without verification, there is no basis for control. Policy and procedures, although closely related and interdependent to a certain extent, are not synonymous. A policy may be adopted, for example, to maintain a materials inventory not to exceed one million dollars. A procedure for inventory control would interpret that policy and convert it into methods for keeping within that limit, with consideration, too, of possible but foreseeable expedient deviation.

4. Procedure
    What is procedure?

    A procedure specifically prescribes:

    a. What work is to be performed by the various participants
    b. Who are the respective participants
    c. When and where the various steps in the different processes are to be performed
    d. The sequence of operations that will insure uniform handling of recurring transactions
    e. The *paper* that is involved, its origin, transition, and disposition

    Necessary appurtenances to a procedure are:

    a. Detailed organizational chart

      b.   Flow charts

      c.   Exhibits of forms, all presented in close proximity to the text of the procedure

5.   <u>Basis of Control - Information in the Hands of Managers</u>
If the basis of control is information in the hands of managers, then <u>reporting</u> is elevated to a level of very considerable importance.

Types of reporting may include:

      a.   Special reports and routine reports
      b.   Written, oral, and graphic reports
      c.   Staff meetings
      d.   Conferences
      e.   Television screens
      f.   Non-receipt of information, as where management is by exception
      g.   Any other means whereby information is transmitted to a manager as a basis for control action

FRAMEWORK OF MANAGEMENT

<u>Elements</u>

1.   <u>Policy</u> - It has to be verified, controlled.

2.   <u>Organization</u> - is part of the giving of an assignment. The organizational chart gives to each individual in his title, a first approximation of the nature of his assignment and orients him as being accountable to a certain individual. Organization is not in a true sense a means of control. Control is checking to ascertain whether the assignment is executed as intended and acting on the basis of that information.

3.   <u>Budgets</u> - perform three functions:

      a.   They present the objectives, plans, and programs of the organization in financial terms.
      b.   They report the progress of actual performance against these predetermined objectives, plans, and programs.
      c.   Like organizational charts, delegations of authority, procedures and job descriptions, they define the assignments which have flowed from the Chief Executive. Budgets are a means of control in the respect that they report progress of actual performance against the program. They provide information which enables managers to take action directed toward bringing actual results into conformity with the program.

4.   <u>Internal Check</u> - provides in practice for the principle that the same person should not have responsibility for all phases of a transaction. This makes it clearly an aspect of organization rather than of control. Internal Check is static, or built-in.

5.   <u>Plans, Programs, Objectives</u>
People must know what they are trying to do. <u>Objectives</u> fulfill this need. Without them, people may work industriously and yet, working aimlessly, accomplish little.

Plans and Programs complement Objectives, since they propose how and according to what time schedule the objectives are to be reached.

6. Delegations of Authority

Among the ways we have for supplementing the titles and lines of authority of an organizational chart are delegations of authority. Delegations of authority clarify the extent of authority of individuals and in that way serve to define assignments. That they are not means of control is apparent from the very fact that wherever there has been a delegation of authority, the need for control increases. This could hardly be expected to happen if delegations of authority were themselves means of control.

Manager's Responsibility

Control becomes necessary whenever a manager delegates authority to a subordinate because he cannot delegate and then simply sit back and forget all about it. A manager's accountability to his own superior has not diminished one whit as a result of delegating part of his authority to a subordinate. The manager must exercise control over actions taken under the authority so delegated. That means checking serves as a basis for possible corrective action.

Objectives, plans, programs, organizational charts, and other elements of the managerial system are not fruitfully regarded as either controls or means of control. They are pre-established standards or models of performance to which operations are adjusted by the exercise of management control. These standards or models of performance are dynamic in character for they are constantly altered, modified, or revised. Policies, organizational set-up, procedures, delegations, etc. are constantly altered but, like objectives and plans, they remain in force until they are either abandoned or revised. All of the elements (or standards or models of performance), objectives, plans and prpgrams, policies, organization, etc. can be regarded as a *framework of management.*

Control Techniques

Examples of control techniques:
1. Compare against established standards
2. Compare with a similar operation
3. Compare with past operations
4. Compare with predictions of accomplishment

Where Forecasts Fit

Control is after-the-fact while forecasts are before. Forecasts and projections are important for setting objectives and formulating plans.

Information for aiming and planning does not have to before-the-fact. It may be an after-the-fact analysis proving that a certain policy has been impolitic in its effect on the relation of the company or department with customer, employee, taxpayer, or stockholder; or that a certain plan is no longer practical, or that a certain procedure is unworkable.

The prescription here certainly would not be in control (in these cases, control would simply bring operations into conformity with obsolete standards) but the establishment of new standards, a new policy, a new plan, and a new procedure to be controlled too.

Information is, of course, the basis for all communication in addition to furnishing evidence to management of the need for reconstructing the framework of management.

PROBLEM SOLVING

The accepted concept in modern management for problem solving is the utilization of the following steps:

1. Identify the problem
2. Gather data
3. List possible solutions
4. Test possible solutions
5. Select the best solution
6. Put the solution into actual practice

Occasions might arise where you would have to apply the second step of gathering data before completing the first step.

You might also find that it will be necessary to work on several steps at the same time.

1. Identify the Problem

Your first step is to define as precisely as possible the problem to be solved. While this may sound easy, it is often the most difficult part of the process.

It has been said of problem solving that you are halfway to the solution when you can write out a clear statement of the problem itself.

Our job now is to get below the surface manifestations of the trouble and pinpoint the problem. This is usually accomplished by a logical analysis, by going from the general to the particular; from the obvious to the not-so-obvious cause.
Let us say that production is behind schedule. WHY? Absenteeism is high. Now, is absenteeism the basic problem to be tackled, or is it merely a symptom of low morale among the workforce? Under these circumstances, you may decide that production is not the problem; the problem is *employee morale*.

In trying to define the problem, remember there is seldom one simple reason why production is lagging, or reports are late, etc.

Analysis usually leads to the discovery that an apparent problem is really made up of several subproblems which must be attacked separately.

Another way is to limit the problem, and thereby ease the task of finding a solution, and concentrate on the elements which are within the scope of your control.

When you have gone this far, write out a tentative statement of the problem to be solved.

2. <u>Gather Data</u>

In the second step, you must set out to collect all the information that might have a bearing on the problem. Do not settle for an assumption when reasonable fact and figures are available.

If you merely go through the motions of problem-solving, you will probably shortcut the information-gathering step. Therefore, do not stack the evidence by confining your research to your own preconceived ideas.

As you collect facts, organize them in some form that helps you make sense of them and spot possible relationships between them. For example: Plotting cost per unit figures on a graph can be more meaningful than a long column of figures.

Evaluate each item as you go along. Is the source material: absolutely reliable, probably reliable, or not to be trusted.

One of the best methods for gathering data is to go out and look the situation over carefully. Talk to the people on the job who are most affected by this problem.

Always keep in mind that a primary source is usually better than a secondary source of information.

3. <u>List Possible Solutions</u>

This is the creative thinking step of problem solving. This is a good time to bring into play whatever techniques of group dynamics the agency or bureau might have developed for a joint attack on problems.

Now the important thing for you to do is: Keep an open mind. Let your imagination roam freely over the facts you have collected. Jot down every possible solution that occurs to you. Resist the temptation to evaluate various proposals as you go along. List seemingly absurd ideas along with more plausible ones. The more possibilities you list during this step, the less risk you will run of settling for merely a workable, rather than the best, solution.

Keep studying the data as long as there seems to be any chance of deriving additional - ideas, solutions, explanations, or patterns from it.

4. <u>Test Possible Solutions</u>

Now you begin to evaluate the possible solutions. Take pains to be objective. Up to this point, you have suspended judgment but you might be tempted to select a solution you secretly favored all along and proclaim it as the best of the lot.

The secret of objectivity in this phase is to test the possible solutions separately, measuring each against a common yardstick. To make this yardstick try to enumerate as many specific criteria as you can think of. Criteria are best phrased as questions which you ask of each possible solution. They can be drawn from these general categories:

Suitability - Will this solution do the job?
Will it solve the problem completely or partially?

Is it a permanent or a stopgap solution?

Feasibility - Will this plan work in actual practice?
Can we afford this approach?
How much will it cost?

Acceptability - Will the boss go along with the changes required in the plan?
Are we trying to drive a tack with a sledge hammer?

5. Select the Best Solution

This is the area of executive decision.

Occasionally, one clearly superior solution will stand out at the conclusion of the testing process. But often it is not that simple. You may find that no one solution has come through all the tests with flying colors.

You may also find that a proposal, which flunked miserably on one of the essential tests, racked up a very high score on others.

The best solution frequently will turn out to be a combination.

Try to arrange a marriage that will bring together the strong points of one possible solution with the particular virtues of another. The more skill and imagination that you apply, the greater is the likelihood that you will come out with a solution that is not merely adequate and workable, but is the best possible under the circumstances.

6. Put the Solution Into Actual Practice
As every executive knows, a plan which works perfectly on paper may develop all sorts of bugs when put into actual practice.

Problem-solving does not stop with selecting the solution which looks best in theory. The next step is to put the chosen solution into action and watch the results. The results may point towards modifications.

If the problem disappears when you put your solution into effect, you know you have the right solution.

If it does not disappear, even after you have adjusted your plan to cover unforeseen difficulties that turned up in practice, work your way back through the problem-solving solutions.

Would one of them have worked better?
Did you overlook some vital piece of data which would have given you a different slant on the whole situation? Did you apply all necessary criteria in testing solutions? If no light dawns after this much rechecking, it is a pretty good bet that you defined the problem incorrectly in the first place.

You came up with the wrong solution because you tackled the wrong problem.

Thus, step six may become step one of a new problem-solving cycle.

COMMUNICATION

1. <u>What is Communication?</u>
   We communicate through writing, speaking, action or inaction. In speaking to people face-to-face, there is opportunity to judge reactions and to adjust the message. This makes the supervisory chain one of the most, and in many instances the most, important channels of communication.

   In an organization, communication means keeping employees informed about the organization's objectives, policies, problems, and progress. Communication is the free interchange of information, ideas, and desirable attitudes between and among employees and between employees and management.

2. <u>Why is Communication Needed?</u>
   a. People have certain social needs
   b. Good communication is essential in meeting those social needs
   c. While people have similar basic needs, at the same time they differ from each other
   d. Communication must be adapted to these individual differences

   An employee cannot do his best work unless he knows why he is doing it. If he has the feeling that he is being kept in the dark about what is going on, his enthusiasm and productivity suffer.

   Effective communication is needed in an organization so that employees will understand what the organization is trying to accomplish; and how the work of one unit contributes to or affects the work of other units in the organization and other organizations.

3. <u>How is Communication Achieved?</u>
   Communication flows downward, upward, sideways.

   a. Communication may come from top management down to employees. This is <u>downward communication</u>.

      Some means of downward communication are:
      (1) Training (orientation, job instruction, supervision, public relations, etc.)
      (2) Conferences
      (3) Staff meetings
      (4) Policy statements
      (5) Bulletins
      (6) Newsletters
      (7) Memoranda
      (8) Circulation of important letters

      In downward communication, it is important that employees be informed in advance of changes that will affect them.

   b. Communications should also be developed so that the ideas, suggestions, and knowledge of employees will flow <u>upward</u> to top management.

Some means of upward communication are:
(1)   Personal discussion conferences
(2)   Committees
(3)   Memoranda
(4)   Employees suggestion program
(5)   Questionnaires to be filled in giving comments and suggestions about proposed actions that will affect field operations

Upward communication requires that management be willing to listen, to accept, and to make changes when good ideas are present. Upward communication succeeds when there is no fear of punishment for speaking out or lack of interest at the top. Employees will share their knowledge and ideas with management when interest is shown and recognition is given.

c.   The *advantages* of downward communication:
   (1)   It enables the passing down of orders, policies, and plans necessary to the continued operation of the station.
   (2)   By making information available, it diminishes the fears and suspicions which result from misinformation and misunderstanding.
   (3)   It fosters the pride people want to have in their work when they are told of good work.
   (4)   It improves the morale and stature of the individual to be *in the know*.
   (5)   It helps employees to understand, accept, and cooperate with changes when they know about them in advance.

d.   The *advantages* of upward communication:
   (1)   It enables the passing upward of information, attitudes, and feelings.
   (2)   It makes it easier to find out how ready people are to receive downward communication.
   (3)   It reveals the degree to which the downward communication is understood and accepted.
   (4)   It helps to satisfy the basic *social* needs.
   (5)   It stimulates employees to participate in the operation of their organization.
   (6)   It encourages employees to contribute ideas for improving the efficiency and economy of operations.
   (7)   It helps to solve problem situations before they reach the explosion point.

4.   Why Does Communication Fail?
   a.   The technical difficulties of conveying information clearly
   b.   The emotional content of communication which prevents complete transmission
   c.   The fact that there is a difference between what management needs to say, what it wants to say, and what it does say
   d.   The fact that there is a difference between what employees would like to say, what they think is profitable or safe to say, and what they do say

5.   How to Improve Communication.
   As a supervisor, you are a key figure in communication. To improve as a communicator, you should:
   a.   Know - Knowing your subordinates will help you to recognize and work with individual differences.

b. <u>Like</u> - If you like those who work for you and those for whom you work, this will foster the kind of friendly, warm, work atmosphere that will facilitate communication.

c. <u>Trust</u> - Showing a sincere desire to communicate will help to develop the mutual trust and confidence which are essential to the free flow of communication.

d. <u>Tell</u> - Tell your subordinates and superiors *what's doing.* Tell your subordinates *why* as well as *how.*

e. <u>Listen</u> - By listening, you help others to talk and you create good listeners. Don't forget that listening implies action.

f. <u>Stimulate</u> - Communication has to be stimulated and encouraged. Be receptive to ideas and suggestions and motivate your people so that each member of the team identifies himself with the job at hand.

g. <u>Consult</u> - The most effective way of consulting is to let your people participate, insofar as possible, in developing determinations which affect them or their work.

6. <u>How to Determine Whether You are Getting Across</u>.
   a. Check to see that communication is received and understood
   b. Judge this understanding by actions rather than words
   c. Adapt or vary communication, when necessary
   d. Remember that good communication cannot cure all problems

7. <u>The Key Attitude</u>.
   Try to see things from the other person's point of view. By doing this, you help to develop the permissive atmosphere and the shared confidence and understanding which are essential to effective two-way communication.

   Communication is a two-way process.
   a. The basic purpose of any communication is to get action.
   b. The only way to get action is through acceptance.
   c. In order to get acceptance, communication must be humanly satisfying as well as technically efficient.

HOW ORDERS AND INSTRUCTIONS SHOULD BE GIVEN

<u>Characteristics of Good Orders and Instructions</u>

1. <u>Clear</u>
   Orders should be definite as to
   - <u>What</u> is to be done
   - <u>Who</u> is to do it
   - <u>When</u> it is to be done
   - <u>Where</u> it is to be done
   - <u>How</u> it is to be done

2. <u>Concise</u>
   Avoid wordiness. Orders should be brief and to the point.

3. <u>Timely</u>
   Instructions and orders should be sent out at the proper time and not too long in advance of expected performance.

4. Possibility of Performance
   Orders should be feasible:
   a. Investigate before giving orders
   b. Consult those who are to carry out instructions before formulating and issuing them

5. Properly Directed
   Give the orders to the people concerned. Do not send orders to people who are not concerned. People who continually receive instructions that are not applicable to them get in the habit of neglecting instructions generally.

6. Reviewed Before Issuance
   Orders should be reviewed before issuance:
   a. Test them by putting yourself in the position of the recipient
   b. If they involve new procedures, have the persons who are to do the work review them for suggestions

7. Reviewed After Issuance
   Persons who receive orders should be allowed to raise questions and to point out unforeseen consequences of orders.

8. Coordinated
   Orders should be coordinated so that work runs smoothly.

9. Courteous
   Make a request rather than a demand. There is no need to continually call attention to the fact that you are the boss.

10. Recognizable as an Order
    Be sure that the order is recognizable as such.

11. Complete
    Be sure recipient has knowledge and experience sufficient to carry out order. Give illustrations and examples.

A DEPARTMENTAL PERSONNEL OFFICE IS RESPONSIBLE FOR THE FOLLOWING FUNCTIONS

1. Policy
2. Personnel Programs
3. Recruitment and Placement
4. Position Classification
5. Salary and Wage Administration
6. Employee Performance Standards and Evaluation
7. Employee Relations
8. Disciplinary Actions and Separations
9. Health and Safety
10. Staff Training and Development
11. Personnel Records, Procedures, and Reports
12. Employee Services
13. Personnel Research

SUPERVISION

Leadership

All leadership is based essentially on authority. This comes from two sources: it is received from higher management or it is earned by the supervisor through his methods of supervision. Although effective leadership has always depended upon the leader's using his authority in such a way as to appeal successfully to the motives of the people supervised, the conditions for making this appeal are continually changing. The key to today's problem of leadership is flexibility and resourcefulness on the part of the leader in meeting changes in conditions as they occur.

Three basic approaches to leadership are generally recognized:

1. The Authoritarian Approach
   a. The methods and techniques used in this approach emphasize the *I* in leadership and depend primarily on the formal authority of the leader. This authority is sometimes exercised in a hardboiled manner and sometimes in a benevolent manner, but in either case the dominating role of the leader is reflected in the thinking, planning, and decisions of the group.
   b. Group results are to a large degree dependent on close supervision by the leader. Usually, the individuals in the group will not show a high degree of initiative or acceptance of responsibility and their capacity to grow and develop probably will not be fully utilized. The group may react with resentment or submission, depending upon the manner and skill of the leader in using his authority
   c. This approach develops as a natural outgrowth of the authority that goes with the leader's job and his feeling of sole responsibility for getting the job done. It is relatively easy to use and does not require much resourcefulness.
   d. The use of this approach is effective in times of emergencies, in meeting close deadlines as a final resort, in settling some issues, in disciplinary matters, and with dependent individuals and groups.

2. The Laissez-Faire or *Let 'em Alone* Approach
   a. This approach generally is characterized by an avoidance of leadership responsibility by the leader. The activities of the group depend largely on the choice of its members rather than the leader.
   b. Group results probably will be poor. Generally, there will be disagreements over petty things, bickering, and confusion. Except for a few aggressive people, individuals will not show much initiative and growth and development will be retarded. There may be a tendency for informal leaders to take over leadership of the group.
   c. This approach frequently results from the leader's dislike of responsibility, from his lack of confidence, from failure of other methods to work, from disappointment or criticism. It is usually the easiest of the three to use and requires both understanding and resourcefulness on the part of the leader.
   d. This approach is occasionally useful and effective, particularly in forcing dependent individuals or groups to rely on themselves, to give someone a chance to save face by clearing his own difficulties, or when action should be delayed temporarily for good cause.

3. <u>The Democratic Approach</u>
   a. The methods and techniques used in this approach emphasize the *we* in leadership and build up the responsibility of the group to attain its objectives. Reliance is placed largely on the earned authority of the leader.
   b. Group results are likely to be good because most of the job motives of the people will be satisfied. Cooperation and teamwork, initiative, acceptance of responsibility, and the individual's capacity for growth probably will show a high degree of development.
   c. This approach grows out of a desire or necessity of the leader to find ways to appeal effectively to the motivation of his group. It is the best approach to build up inside the person a strong desire to cooperate and apply himself to the job.
      It is the most difficult to develop, and requires both understanding and resourcefulness on the part of the leader.
   d. The value of this approach increases over a long period where sustained efficiency and development of people are important. It may not be fully effective in all situations, however, particularly when there is not sufficient time to use it properly or where quick decisions must be made.

All three approaches are used by most leaders and have a place in supervising people. The extent of their use varies with individual leaders, with some using one approach predominantly. The leader who uses these three approaches, and varies their use with time and circumstance, is probably the most effective. Leadership which is used predominantly with a democratic approach requires more resourcefulness on the part of the leader but offers the greatest possibilities in terms of teamwork and cooperation.

The one best way of developing democratic leadership is to provide a real sense of participation on the part of the group, since this satisfies most of the chief job motives. Although there are many ways of providing participation, consulting as frequently as possible with individuals and groups on things that affect them seems to offer the most in building cooperation and responsibility. Consultation takes different forms, but it is most constructive when people feel they are actually helping in finding the answers to the problems on the job.

There are some requirements of leaders in respect to human relations which should be considered in their selection and development. Generally, the leader should be interested in working with other people, emotionally stable, self-confident, and sensitive to the reactions of others. In addition, his viewpoint should be one of getting the job done through people who work cooperatively in response to his leadership. He should have a knowledge of individual and group behavior, but, most important of all, he should work to combine all of these requirements into a definite, practical skill in leadership.

<u>Nine Points of Contrast Between *Boss* and *Leader*</u>

1. The boss drives his men; the leader coaches them.
2. The boss depends on authority; the leader on good will.
3. The boss inspires fear; the leader inspires enthusiasm.
4. The boss says J; the leader says *We*.
5. The boss says *Get here on time;* the leader gets there ahead of time.
6. The boss fixes the blame for the breakdown; the leader fixes the breakdown.
7. The boss knows how it is done; the leader shows how.
8. The boss makes work a drudgery; the leader makes work a game.
9. The boss says *Go*; the leader says *Let's go.*

EMPLOYEE MORALE

Employee morale is the way employees feel about each other, the organization or unit in which they work, and the work they perform.

Some Ways to Develop and Maintain Good Employee Morale

1. Give adequate credit and praise when due.
2. Recognize importance of all jobs and equalize load with proper assignments, always giving consideration to personality differences and abilities.
3. Welcome suggestions and do not have an *all-wise* attitude. Request employees' assistance in solving problems and use assistants when conducting group meetings on certain subjects.
4. Properly assign responsibilities and give adequate authority for fulfillment of such assignments.
5. Keep employees informed about matters that affect them.
6. Criticize and reprimand employees privately.
7. Be accessible and willing to listen.
8. Be fair.
9. Be alert to detect training possibilities so that you will not miss an opportunity to help each employee do a better job, and if possible with less effort on his part.
10. Set a good example.
11. Apply the golden rule.

Some Indicators of Good Morale
1. Good quality of work
2. Good quantity
3. Good attitude of employees
4. Good discipline
5. Teamwork
6. Good attendance
7. Employee participation

MOTIVATION

Drives

A *drive,* stated simply, is a desire or force which causes a person to do or say certain things. These are some of the most usual drives and some of their identifying characteristics recognizable in people motivated by such drives:

1. Security (desire to provide for the future)
   Always on time for work
   Works for the same employer for many years
   Never takes unnecessary chances Seldom resists doing what he is told

2. Recognition (desire to be rewarded for accomplishment)
   Likes to be asked for his opinion
   Becomes very disturbed when he makes a mistake
   Does things to attract attention

Likes to see his name in print

3. Position (desire to hold certain status in relation to others)
    Boasts about important people he knows
    Wants to be known as a key man
    Likes titles
    Demands respect
    Belongs to clubs, for prestige

4. Accomplishment (desire to get things done)
    Complains when things are held up
    Likes to do things that have tangible results
    Never lies down on the job
    Is proud of turning out good work

5. Companionship (desire to associate with other people)
    Likes to work with others
    Tells stories and jokes
    Indulges in horseplay
    Finds excuses to talk to others on the job

6. Possession (desire to collect and hoard objects)
    Likes to collect things
    Puts his name on things belonging to him
    Insists on the same work location

Supervisors may find that identifying the drives of employees is a helpful step toward motivating them to self-improvement and better job performance. For example: An employee's job performance is below average. His supervisor, having previously determined that the employee is motivated by a drive for security, suggests that taking training courses will help the employee to improve, advance, and earn more money. Since earning more money can be a step toward greater security, the employee's drive for security would motivate him to take the training suggested by the supervisor. In essence, this is the process of charting an employee's future course by using his motivating drives to positive advantage.

EMPLOYEE PARTICIPATION

What is Participation?

Employee participation is the employee's giving freely of his time, skill and knowledge to an extent which cannot be obtained by demand.

Why is it Important?

The supervisor's responsibility is to get the job done through people. A good supervisor gets the job done through people who work willingly and well. The participation of employees is important because:

1. Employees develop a greater sense of responsibility when they share in working out operating plans and goals.
2. Participation provides greater opportunity and stimulation for employees to learn, and to develop their ability.

3. Participation sometimes provides better solutions to problems because such solutions may combine the experience and knowledge of interested employees who want the solutions to work.
4. An employee or group may offer a solution which the supervisor might hesitate to make for fear of demanding too much.
5. Since the group wants to make the solution work, they exert *pressure* in a constructive way on each other.
6. Participation usually results in reducing the need for close supervision.

How May Supervisors Obtain It?

Participation is encouraged when employees feel that they share some responsibility for the work and that their ideas are sincerely wanted and valued. Some ways of obtaining employee participation are:

1. Conduct orientation programs for new employees to inform them about the organization and their rights and responsibilities as employees.
2. Explain the aims and objectives of the agency. On a continuing basis, be sure that the employees know what these aims and objectives are.
3. Share job successes and responsibilities and give credit for success.
4. Consult with employees, both as individuals and in groups, about things that affect them.
5. Encourage suggestions for job improvements. Help employees to develop good suggestions. The suggestions can bring them recognition. The city's suggestion program offers additional encouragement through cash awards.

The supervisor who encourages employee participation is not surrendering his authority. He must still make decisions and initiate action, and he must continue to be ultimately responsible for the work of those he supervises. But, through employee participation, he is helping his group to develop greater ability and a sense of responsibility while getting the job done faster and better.

STEPS IN HANDLING A GRIEVANCE

1. Get the facts
   a. Listen sympathetically.
   b. Let him talk himself out.
   c. Get his story straight.
   d. Get his point of view.
   e. Don't argue with him.
   f. Give him plenty of time.
   g. Conduct the interview privately.
   h. Don't try to shift the blame or pass the buck.

2. Consider the facts
   a. Consider the employee's viewpoint.
   b. How will the decision affect similar cases.
   c. Consider each decision as a possible precedent.
   d. Avoid snap judgments - don't jump to conclusions.

3. <u>Make or get a decision</u>
    a. Frame an effective counter-proposal.
    b. Make sure it is fair to all.
    c. Have confidence in your judgment.
    d. Be sure you can substantiate your decision.

4. <u>Notify the employee of your decision</u>
    Be sure he is told; try to convince him that the decision is fair and just.

5. <u>Take action when needed and if within your authority</u>
    Otherwise, tell employee that the matter will be called to the attention of the proper person or that nothing can be done, and why it cannot.

6. <u>Follow through</u> to see that the desired result is achieved.

7. <u>Record key facts</u> concerning the complaint and the action taken.

8. <u>Leave the way open to him to appeal your decision</u> to a higher authority.

9. <u>Report all grievances to your superior</u>, whether they are appealed or not.

DISCIPLINE

Discipline is training that develops self-control, orderly conduct, and efficiency.

To discipline does not necessarily mean to punish.

To discipline does mean to train, to regulate, and to govern conduct.

The Disciplinary Interview

Most employees sincerely want to do what is expected of them. In other words, they are self-disciplined. Some employees, however, fail to observe established rules and standards, and disciplinary action by the supervisor is required.

The primary purpose of disciplinary action is to improve conduct without creating dissatisfaction, bitterness, or resentment in the process.

Constructive disciplinary action is more concerned with causes and explanations of breaches of conduct than with punishment. The disciplinary interview is held to get at the causes of apparent misbehavior and to motivate better performance in the future.

It is important that the interview be kept on as impersonal a basis as possible. If the supervisor lets the interview descend to the plane of an argument, it loses its effectiveness.

Planning the Interview

Get all pertinent facts concerning the situation so that you can talk in specific terms to the employee.

Review the employee's record, appraisal ratings, etc.

Consider what you know about the temperament of the employee. Consider your attitude toward the employee. Remember that the primary requisite of disciplinary action is fairness.

Don't enter upon the interview when angry.

Schedule the interview for a place which is private and out of hearing of others.

Conducting the Interview

1. Make an effort to establish accord.

2. Question the employee about the apparent breach of discipline. Be sure that the question is not so worded as to be itself an accusation.

3. Give the employee a chance to tell his side of the story. Give him ample opportunity to talk.

4. Use understanding-listening except where it is necessary to ask a question or to point out some details of which the employee may not be aware. If the employee misrepresents facts, make a plain, accurate statement of the facts, but don't argue and don't engage in personal controversy.

5. Listen and try to understand the reasons for the employee's (mis)conduct. First of all, don't assume that there has been a breach of discipline. Evaluate the employee's reasons for his conduct in the light of his opinions and feelings concerning the consistency and reasonableness of the standards which he was expected to follow. Has the supervisor done his part in explaining the reasons for the rules? Was the employee's behavior unintentional or deliberate? Does he think he had real reasons for his actions? What new facts is he telling? Do the facts justify his actions? What causes, other than those mentioned, could have stimulated the behavior?

6. After listening to the employee's version of the situation, and if censure of his actions is warranted, the supervisor should proceed with whatever criticism is justified. Emphasis should be placed on future improvement rather than exclusively on the employee's failure to measure up to expected standards of job conduct.

7. Fit the criticism to the individual. With one employee, a word of correction may be all that is required.

8. Attempt to distinguish between unintentional error and deliberate misbehavior. An error due to ignorance requires training and not censure.

9. Administer criticism in a controlled, even tone of voice, never in anger. Make it clear that you are acting as an agent of the department. In general, criticism should refer to the job or the employee's actions and not to the person. Criticism of the employee's work is not an attack on the individual.

10. Be sure the interview does not destroy the employee's self-confidence. Mention his good qualities and assure him that you feel confident that he can improve his performance.

11. Wherever possible, before the employee leaves the interview, satisfy him that the incident is closed, that nothing more will be said on the subject unless the offense is repeated.

———

ANSWER SHEET

TEST NO. ______________ PART ______ TITLE OF POSITION ______________________________
(AS GIVEN IN EXAMINATION ANNOUNCEMENT - INCLUDE OPTION, IF ANY)

PLACE OF EXAMINATION ______________________________ (CITY OR TOWN) ______________ (STATE) DATE ______________

RATING

USE THE SPECIAL PENCIL. MAKE GLOSSY BLACK MARKS.

1	A B C D E	26	A B C D E	51	A B C D E	76	A B C D E	101	A B C D E
2	A B C D E	27	A B C D E	52	A B C D E	77	A B C D E	102	A B C D E
3	A B C D E	28	A B C D E	53	A B C D E	78	A B C D E	103	A B C D E
4	A B C D E	29	A B C D E	54	A B C D E	79	A B C D E	104	A B C D E
5	A B C D E	30	A B C D E	55	A B C D E	80	A B C D E	105	A B C D E
6	A B C D E	31	A B C D E	56	A B C D E	81	A B C D E	106	A B C D E
7	A B C D E	32	A B C D E	57	A B C D E	82	A B C D E	107	A B C D E
8	A B C D E	33	A B C D E	58	A B C D E	83	A B C D E	108	A B C D E
9	A B C D E	34	A B C D E	59	A B C D E	84	A B C D E	109	A B C D E
10	A B C D E	35	A B C D E	60	A B C D E	85	A B C D E	110	A B C D E

Make only ONE mark for each answer. Additional and stray marks may be counted as mistakes. In making corrections, erase errors COMPLETELY.

11	A B C D E	36	A B C D E	61	A B C D E	86	A B C D E	111	A B C D E
12	A B C D E	37	A B C D E	62	A B C D E	87	A B C D E	112	A B C D E
13	A B C D E	38	A B C D E	63	A B C D E	88	A B C D E	113	A B C D E
14	A B C D E	39	A B C D E	64	A B C D E	89	A B C D E	114	A B C D E
15	A B C D E	40	A B C D E	65	A B C D E	90	A B C D E	115	A B C D E
16	A B C D E	41	A B C D E	66	A B C D E	91	A B C D E	116	A B C D E
17	A B C D E	42	A B C D E	67	A B C D E	92	A B C D E	117	A B C D E
18	A B C D E	43	A B C D E	68	A B C D E	93	A B C D E	118	A B C D E
19	A B C D E	44	A B C D E	69	A B C D E	94	A B C D E	119	A B C D E
20	A B C D E	45	A B C D E	70	A B C D E	95	A B C D E	120	A B C D E
21	A B C D E	46	A B C D E	71	A B C D E	96	A B C D E	121	A B C D E
22	A B C D E	47	A B C D E	72	A B C D E	97	A B C D E	122	A B C D E
23	A B C D E	48	A B C D E	73	A B C D E	98	A B C D E	123	A B C D E
24	A B C D E	49	A B C D E	74	A B C D E	99	A B C D E	124	A B C D E
25	A B C D E	50	A B C D E	75	A B C D E	100	A B C D E	125	A B C D E

ANSWER SHEET

TEST NO. _____ PART _____ TITLE OF POSITION _____

(AS GIVEN IN EXAMINATION ANNOUNCEMENT - INCLUDE OPTION. IF ANY)

PLACE OF EXAMINATION _____ DATE _____

(CITY OR TOWN)   (STATE)

RATING

USE THE SPECIAL PENCIL.   MAKE GLOSSY BLACK MARKS.

	A	B	C	D	E		A	B	C	D	E		A	B	C	D	E		A	B	C	D	E		A	B	C	D	E
1	⋮	⋮	⋮	⋮	⋮	26	⋮	⋮	⋮	⋮	⋮	51	⋮	⋮	⋮	⋮	⋮	76	⋮	⋮	⋮	⋮	⋮	101	⋮	⋮	⋮	⋮	⋮
2	⋮	⋮	⋮	⋮	⋮	27	⋮	⋮	⋮	⋮	⋮	52	⋮	⋮	⋮	⋮	⋮	77	⋮	⋮	⋮	⋮	⋮	102	⋮	⋮	⋮	⋮	⋮
3	⋮	⋮	⋮	⋮	⋮	28	⋮	⋮	⋮	⋮	⋮	53	⋮	⋮	⋮	⋮	⋮	78	⋮	⋮	⋮	⋮	⋮	103	⋮	⋮	⋮	⋮	⋮
4	⋮	⋮	⋮	⋮	⋮	29	⋮	⋮	⋮	⋮	⋮	54	⋮	⋮	⋮	⋮	⋮	79	⋮	⋮	⋮	⋮	⋮	104	⋮	⋮	⋮	⋮	⋮
5	⋮	⋮	⋮	⋮	⋮	30	⋮	⋮	⋮	⋮	⋮	55	⋮	⋮	⋮	⋮	⋮	80	⋮	⋮	⋮	⋮	⋮	105	⋮	⋮	⋮	⋮	⋮
6	⋮	⋮	⋮	⋮	⋮	31	⋮	⋮	⋮	⋮	⋮	56	⋮	⋮	⋮	⋮	⋮	81	⋮	⋮	⋮	⋮	⋮	106	⋮	⋮	⋮	⋮	⋮
7	⋮	⋮	⋮	⋮	⋮	32	⋮	⋮	⋮	⋮	⋮	57	⋮	⋮	⋮	⋮	⋮	82	⋮	⋮	⋮	⋮	⋮	107	⋮	⋮	⋮	⋮	⋮
8	⋮	⋮	⋮	⋮	⋮	33	⋮	⋮	⋮	⋮	⋮	58	⋮	⋮	⋮	⋮	⋮	83	⋮	⋮	⋮	⋮	⋮	108	⋮	⋮	⋮	⋮	⋮
9	⋮	⋮	⋮	⋮	⋮	34	⋮	⋮	⋮	⋮	⋮	59	⋮	⋮	⋮	⋮	⋮	84	⋮	⋮	⋮	⋮	⋮	109	⋮	⋮	⋮	⋮	⋮
10	⋮	⋮	⋮	⋮	⋮	35	⋮	⋮	⋮	⋮	⋮	60	⋮	⋮	⋮	⋮	⋮	85	⋮	⋮	⋮	⋮	⋮	110	⋮	⋮	⋮	⋮	⋮

Make only ONE mark for each answer.   Additional and stray marks may be
counted as mistakes.   In making corrections, erase errors COMPLETELY.

	A	B	C	D	E		A	B	C	D	E		A	B	C	D	E		A	B	C	D	E		A	B	C	D	E
11	⋮	⋮	⋮	⋮	⋮	36	⋮	⋮	⋮	⋮	⋮	61	⋮	⋮	⋮	⋮	⋮	86	⋮	⋮	⋮	⋮	⋮	111	⋮	⋮	⋮	⋮	⋮
12	⋮	⋮	⋮	⋮	⋮	37	⋮	⋮	⋮	⋮	⋮	62	⋮	⋮	⋮	⋮	⋮	87	⋮	⋮	⋮	⋮	⋮	112	⋮	⋮	⋮	⋮	⋮
13	⋮	⋮	⋮	⋮	⋮	38	⋮	⋮	⋮	⋮	⋮	63	⋮	⋮	⋮	⋮	⋮	88	⋮	⋮	⋮	⋮	⋮	113	⋮	⋮	⋮	⋮	⋮
14	⋮	⋮	⋮	⋮	⋮	39	⋮	⋮	⋮	⋮	⋮	64	⋮	⋮	⋮	⋮	⋮	89	⋮	⋮	⋮	⋮	⋮	114	⋮	⋮	⋮	⋮	⋮
15	⋮	⋮	⋮	⋮	⋮	40	⋮	⋮	⋮	⋮	⋮	65	⋮	⋮	⋮	⋮	⋮	90	⋮	⋮	⋮	⋮	⋮	115	⋮	⋮	⋮	⋮	⋮
16	⋮	⋮	⋮	⋮	⋮	41	⋮	⋮	⋮	⋮	⋮	66	⋮	⋮	⋮	⋮	⋮	91	⋮	⋮	⋮	⋮	⋮	116	⋮	⋮	⋮	⋮	⋮
17	⋮	⋮	⋮	⋮	⋮	42	⋮	⋮	⋮	⋮	⋮	67	⋮	⋮	⋮	⋮	⋮	92	⋮	⋮	⋮	⋮	⋮	117	⋮	⋮	⋮	⋮	⋮
18	⋮	⋮	⋮	⋮	⋮	43	⋮	⋮	⋮	⋮	⋮	68	⋮	⋮	⋮	⋮	⋮	93	⋮	⋮	⋮	⋮	⋮	118	⋮	⋮	⋮	⋮	⋮
19	⋮	⋮	⋮	⋮	⋮	44	⋮	⋮	⋮	⋮	⋮	69	⋮	⋮	⋮	⋮	⋮	94	⋮	⋮	⋮	⋮	⋮	119	⋮	⋮	⋮	⋮	⋮
20	⋮	⋮	⋮	⋮	⋮	45	⋮	⋮	⋮	⋮	⋮	70	⋮	⋮	⋮	⋮	⋮	95	⋮	⋮	⋮	⋮	⋮	120	⋮	⋮	⋮	⋮	⋮
21	⋮	⋮	⋮	⋮	⋮	46	⋮	⋮	⋮	⋮	⋮	71	⋮	⋮	⋮	⋮	⋮	96	⋮	⋮	⋮	⋮	⋮	121	⋮	⋮	⋮	⋮	⋮
22	⋮	⋮	⋮	⋮	⋮	47	⋮	⋮	⋮	⋮	⋮	72	⋮	⋮	⋮	⋮	⋮	97	⋮	⋮	⋮	⋮	⋮	122	⋮	⋮	⋮	⋮	⋮
23	⋮	⋮	⋮	⋮	⋮	48	⋮	⋮	⋮	⋮	⋮	73	⋮	⋮	⋮	⋮	⋮	98	⋮	⋮	⋮	⋮	⋮	123	⋮	⋮	⋮	⋮	⋮
24	⋮	⋮	⋮	⋮	⋮	49	⋮	⋮	⋮	⋮	⋮	74	⋮	⋮	⋮	⋮	⋮	99	⋮	⋮	⋮	⋮	⋮	124	⋮	⋮	⋮	⋮	⋮
25	⋮	⋮	⋮	⋮	⋮	50	⋮	⋮	⋮	⋮	⋮	75	⋮	⋮	⋮	⋮	⋮	100	⋮	⋮	⋮	⋮	⋮	125	⋮	⋮	⋮	⋮	⋮